Lamenting the Pandemic Season

Lamenting the Pandemic Season

—— Journal-Keeping with Bible Verses and Prayers ——

Gwendolyn Carole Tipton

RESOURCE *Publications* · Eugene, Oregon

LAMENTING THE PANDEMIC SEASON
Journal-Keeping with Bible Verses and Prayers

Resource Publications
An Imprint of Wipf and Stock Publishers
199 W. 8th Ave., Suite 3
Eugene, OR 97401

www.wipfandstock.com

PAPERBACK ISBN: 978-1-6667-5647-0
HARDCOVER ISBN: 978-1-6667-5648-7
EBOOK ISBN: 978-1-6667-5649-4

02/17/23

For my beloved granddaughter, Mila Quinn,
who was born in February 2020,
approximately one month before COVID-19
was declared a pandemic.

Contents

Preface

I T IS QUITE POSSIBLE that King David kept a journal that ultimately became part of the Psalms. He wrote about what was happening in his surroundings and his feelings related to those life events. The Psalms describe his thoughts and prayers that help understand it all. He wrote songs of praise to express his gratitude for God. David's Psalms of lament spoke of his sorrowfulness and pain when he was unhappy. His words of thanksgiving clearly said "thank you" in many ways. David differentiated between the wise and the wicked and frequently asked God to help them both. In the royal Psalms, David prays for other kings. In most Psalms, there are prayers of supplication petitioning God for help or intervention.

Lamenting the Pandemic Season is my book of psalms. It expresses my deepest feelings and thoughts on the pandemic season. It includes Bible verses to support my commentary and prayers to God for help.

When I first learned the coronavirus set foot in the US, I began journaling about the pandemic, how I saw it, and how it impacted our lives. My recent journal started in February 2020. Two years later, in spring 2022, the pandemic dissipated in much of the world. Over the past two years, my life has changed. I don't do the things I used to do. My church does not hold regular services or activities, and my women's club meets via Zoom.

Daily newspapers have said the pandemic is over. But what's left is troubling. More than a million Americans have succumbed to COVID-19. The Center for Disease Control and Prevention (CDC) has found millions more filled with depression and anxiety. Millions are suffering from substance abuse, domestic abuse, and mental disorders.

Every day, I wrote in my journal as I listened to and watched news commentators' reports on COVID-19. This book includes thoughts, feelings, and prayers from my journal. I could say I'm burned out, but reality says burnout has not occurred. Instead, my life changes remain permanently in my heart and mind.

I've written four books, and I had planned to travel cross country, host book signings in local bookstores, and promote journaling, which is the focus of my most recent book, *Journal It: Take Hold of Your Life by Journaling*. Unfortunately, my husband had a traumatic brain injury, a heart-related issue, a series of mini-strokes, and one acute one. I scuttled the plan and became a full-time caregiver. Other writers and publishing professionals asked why I didn't devise another plan to promote my book. I said I tried but failed miserably. I blame it on my lack of time to focus and the need to be a 24/7 caregiver.

The pandemic is somewhat over. I survived COVID-19 and am among the living. Yet, COVID-19 got me. After a Wednesday afternoon visit, our daughter took our granddaughter to the doctor on Friday and learned that she had an ear infection and CO-VID-19. After that exposure, Grandpa and I tested positive and were quarantined for one week since we had the two Pfizer vaccines. We surmised that we contracted it from our two-year-old granddaughter, who caught it from her father.

Grandpa had a mild cough, and my body ached all over. After about a week, we both felt better. Now we're boosted and wearing masks. Our frequent destinations are doctor's offices, hospitals, and labs. All of which require cover. The pandemic taught me to shop online and pick up my groceries, and I'm continuing that procedure. When I stop along the way, I'm amazed that no one has a mask. I stand out because I am still wearing one.

President Biden and the CDC said we could take off our masks. Therefore, it must be over. Biden's first State of the Union speech said, "Tonight I can say we are moving forward safely, back to more normal routines . . . It's time for Americans to get back to work and fill our great downtown areas again."[1]

Like today, the pandemic of 1918 ended in two years when people stopped wearing masks and got on with their lives. The influenza strain behind the 1918 pandemic became less life-threatening within a few years. Scientists say this is likely due to herd immunity and the virus mutating to produce a less severe illness. The 1918 influenza strain never disappeared. Instead, scientists believe it continued to mutate, and a version of it circulates today.

Historically, most pandemics end within two to three years as the virus mutates less and the population builds immunity. Scientists explain this may happen with the coronavirus. It is unknown whether it happens with Omicron, a variant that appears to cause milder infections, or another future variant. I am not sure what this means for us.

Every day, I wrote and watched news commentators tell the COVID-19 stories. This book compiles my entries that share my thoughts, feelings, and prayers.

I approached writing differently for my self-indoctrinated reasons and seasons. At the beginning of this book, I try to convince you to journal with a few basic tenets. Join me in journaling your journey through the pandemic. I write daily. This book is part of my journey with prayer during the pandemic.

1. Biden, Joe, "State of the Union Address" (Whitehouse.gov, Mar 1, 2022, https://www.whitehouse.gov/briefing-room/speeches-remarks/2022/03/01/remarks-of-president-joe-biden-state-of-the-union-address-as-delivered).

Introduction

WHAT WERE YOU DOING with all your thoughts and emotions during the incredible COVID-19 days? Never have we watched so much TV news and so many YouTube videos. Nor have we been so impacted by scientists, professors, previous government personnel, and those needing a viral video to add to their résumés. We're learning new words from doctors, legal advisers, and interviewers. Our psyches are trying to understand what we'll do with all this information.

At the beginning of chapter 1, there are thoughts about journaling from my perspective, where I discuss the benefits of journaling and urge you to pray while expressing all your timely experiences in print. Throughout this book, I continue to advise readers about journaling while I share my thoughts, activities, and prayers, thereby composing a mishmash of information.

Journal it! Memorialize these COVID-19 days by journaling in real-time as change happens. Tragically, in nearly 125 days, almost five million people in the US have contracted this coronavirus, and almost two hundred thousand people have died. Simultaneously, millions protested for police reform and better human relations for African Americans, Latinos, Asian Americans, and the LGBTQ community.

Change is occurring in our lives and around the globe dangerously fast. Who are we going to be when these strange times end?

We can fill our daily journals with notes, memorabilia, news clippings, video streaming, and environmental comments.

Educators should direct every youngster who can write or talk to memorialize what's happening. Their senses process new sights, sounds, touches, smells, and tastes. Writing about these impressions will help train youngsters for their next phase of life. Indeed, this is true for all of us.

The Spanish Flu of 1918 ended in 1920, when there was collective immunity, despite the virus being never-ending. Scientists will say the virus has ended when there are no uncontrolled community transmission and only superficial cases.

Following the pandemic, survivors found the Roaring Twenties filled with euphoria and a stable economy. Despite Prohibition, alcohol flourished, making millionaires and criminals. The era birthed a new woman with short hair and a short skirt who could vote. Clashes emerged between the young and old about jazz music and living in urban areas. Also, the cultural civil war started with the migration of African Americans from the South, displaying a novel culture of jazz and blues, along with the literary giants of the Harlem Renaissance. At the same time, the Ku Klux Klan was expanding and intimidating black communities with support from Jim Crow laws.

Perhaps we can look forward to a booming bastion post-COVID-19? Like Prohibition, some states and counties allow marijuana and create millionaires and criminals. This era is generating new employees who choose to work from home and will work where it's convenient for them. Clashes between Republicans and Democrats are creating new political wings within the parties. Our current cultural wars are between races and immigrants, while white supremacists are expanding the beliefs of the Ku Klux Klan. It sounds like 1920 reinvented.

Can you imagine perusing your great-grandparents' journal during the Spanish Flu and the Roaring Twenties? As we begin journaling, our grandchildren will visualize history intimately while learning more about Grandma or Grandpa than they ever expected to share.

CHAPTER 1

Journaling Inspirations, Bible Verses, and Prayers

"Preoccupied with news while staying home,
I watched justice and injustice return
from around the world wailing with bemoan."

Journal It! Take Hold of Your Life by Journaling

J OURNAL IT AND TAKE hold to change your life going forward. You need only a writing instrument and paper on which to write a journal and the commitment to yourself that you will journal. If you are dedicated, you will experiment until you establish a pace and place that feels good and demands that you write something at an appointed time.

And pray . . . Heavenly Father, take and receive my whole life, all I am and want to be. You made me. Now take me back and use me according to your will. Give me the tenacity and discipline to follow through so that ultimately, you will "create in me a pure heart, O God, and renew a steadfast spirit within me" (Ps 51:10). Amen. February 2020.

Journaling—Using the Bible

Throughout the Bible, we are encouraged to write down things. Writing your vision as a first step in taking hold of your life by

3

journaling is essential. In Habakkuk, the prophet complained to the Lord and asked for help because of the wickedness that surrounded him. He was looking for justice for the wrongdoers. Because he believed and trusted in the Lord, Habakkuk knew the Lord had the answer to his problem. The Lord responded, "Look at the nations and watch—and be utterly amazed. For I am going to do something in your days that you would not believe, even if you were told" (Hab 1:5).

Habakkuk complained again about men destroying the nation. The Lord replied, "Write down the revelation and make it plain on tablets so that a herald may run with it. The revelation awaits an appointed time; it speaks of the end and will not prove false. Though it lingers, wait for it; it will certainly come and will not delay" (Hab 2:2–3).

When our lives are not going as we like and we're suffering, we call on the Lord, asking for help and an end to the pain. In this anguish, there is the meaning and always something to be learned. When the Lord answered Habakkuk the second time, he gained hope because of the answer to write down this information so that somebody could share it with others.

The Lord will meet us where we are as we stand in silence while we write and watch him work and witness his glory in action in our lives and those around us.

God revealed the big picture, and Habakkuk didn't quite get it. But he knew that no matter what, God says, "The righteous will live by his faith" (Hab 2:4). So what do you want to write? Where are you going? What would you like to achieve with your journal?

Prayer: Heavenly Father, we promise to write our thoughts in a journal. Help us to reset our priorities and perhaps give up some other activities. We will set time for you alone to write our messages of gratitude, love, and praise. Please know our purpose for journaling is to ask for the pandemic to end. We don't know what to request but ask the Holy Spirit to pray for us to have better lives worldwide. Show us your glory, Lord. Amen. March 2020.

Journaling Can Be helpful

Journal writing can be helpful when you're stuck in emotional conditions. Consider these descriptive words as they may remind you of some feelings.

Strain—I consider anxiety when I feel overwhelmed, and constant worry keeps me from sleeping. My daughter, who has multiple sclerosis, was having her first baby at age 42. We've made it to week 38, and she's exhausted. I began writing prayers about my concerns each night until I fell asleep. During the next week, Mila was born, weighing 6.9 pounds. The daughter and granddaughter are both doing well.

Sorrow—I feel sadness and grief when writing about my brother's affliction. Good conversation and smiles mask his pain. Since serving in the military, he has suffered from a sickness that requires daily dialysis. Recently, a stroke and other complications brought on blindness. I have a section devoted to praying for his healing in my daily journal.

When I saw him last Sunday, his positive spirit sent me to write a praise report in my journal. Colossians says: "Set your minds on things above, not earthly things." There is limited research literature on journaling. However, therapeutic journaling is becoming useful for psychologists and school counselors. Journaling can help you get over an adverse event. Journaling can help you recover from good or bad occurrences in many creative and effective ways.

Prayer: Heavenly Father, I am writing to my readers to encourage them to write reflections from you to help them transform their lives. Guide me as I speak words that may reveal your messages. Thank you for the opportunity to share your word. Amen. March 2020.

Journaling during COVID-19

If there was a time to create a particular journal, it is now, during the pandemic. Journal writing can help us get through these days of being stationary as we have never endured before. Consider these new phrases and different words as they may prod us to make specific moves. Before we start journaling, let's get some information about COVID-19.

The worldwide coronavirus COVID-19 outbreak has officially been declared a pandemic by the World Health Organization (WHO). The director-general of WHO stated, "WHO has been assessing this outbreak around the clock and we are deeply concerned both by the alarming levels of spread and severity, and by the alarming levels of inaction. We have therefore made the assessment that COVID-19 can be characterized as a pandemic."[1] A pandemic is the worldwide spread of a new disease between countries and continents.

Social distancing, shelter in place, and self-quarantine are phrases in the public media. Social distancing is deliberately expanding the physical space around you and the persons near you. Scientists say that staying at least six feet away from other people decreases your odds of getting COVID-19. This expression commands avoiding any crowd, whether at work, school, family gatherings, or conferences. Canceling events where massive groups congregate is a consequence of social distancing.

Shelter in place during this pandemic means taking refuge wherever you are staying, except for necessary trips related to healthcare, food, and essential travel to work. Health organizations use this phrase during natural disasters. In this manner, we're alluding to the coronavirus as a disastrous event. Some call it warfare with an invisible enemy. The US government instructs its citizens who are in foreign countries to get home or shelter in place.

Self-quarantine is for individuals exposed to the coronavirus and who might be in danger of catching it. Self-quarantine involves staying at home, not having guests, remaining at least six feet away from others in your household, not sharing utensils or towels, and

---

1. "WHO Director-General's opening remarks at the media briefing on COVID-19" (World Health Organization, Mar 11, 2020, https://www.who.int/director-general/speeches/detail/who-director-general-s-opening-remarks-at-the-media-briefing-on-covid-19---11-march-2020), paras. 6–7.

washing your hands frequently for fourteen days. Then, ask your doctor for information on how to return to your daily routine.

Prayer: Heavenly Father, I am writing to my readers to encourage them to write their thoughts of petition, meditation, and remembrance to help us with overcoming the coronavirus that is spreading far and wide around the world. Guide us as we write about things happening in our lives with the abrupt changes in our comings and goings and our feelings about now being still. We put ourselves in your hands, knowing that you are the Great Physician with healing powers. Thank you for caring about us. Amen. March 2020.

Journaling While at Home During COVID-19

Our lives will never be the same. Journaling will help us get through the days ahead and remember the past. I introduced COVID-19 with some basic information. Now I want to share my writings and pray they give you cause and encouragement to write in your journal. In recent mornings I awaken with thoughts of how the day will be different because I have no excursions, not even errands to run, and absolutely no concrete destinations. I get through the day and listen to the media promise a better tomorrow. Writing about this season is to journal the happenings as they seem unbelievable.

My life is changing, and I am not at the helm of the transformation. Today, my friend who is not spiritual said, "I believe God is in the mix of this reality." We continued with a dialogue that covered if we have time and space to change our lives. We're committed to staying in place and doing it with no distance breaks. We've built new teams, and we're playing old games. And we're discovering what it's like to be with our children and cohabiters all day when it's not a fun-filled vacation. Although I have no critical place to go, I am an essential person as defined by this coronavirus season because I am a caregiver for my spouse, who is recovering from a traumatic brain injury. There are only two of us in our home. He sleeps two-thirds of the day and is wakeful around mealtimes.

I connect to reality through television and websites. I've figured out how to make this work for me while I write and work on projects around the house. Then, before I know it, it's time to go to sleep, and another day comes. Before COVID-19, my day-to-day schedule was straightforward, with weekends interspersed with attending church and maybe dinner with family and friends. Now it's commanded by the governor's stay-at-home mandate. The rest of the state residents have joined my simple life, which may be a problem for them, perhaps for you.

If I were you, I would become the house chief and plan to involve everyone in creative activities. They don't have to realize that you have a strategy. It would help if you moved them throughout the day so it is easy for everyone to explore the borders of the home space. Write positive and negative happenings and plan a tomorrow that overcomes the flaws and enhances the positives of the past day.

Writing in a journal will help you manage your daily movements while remaining close to each other. And the journal must include what's happening in the world.

I want to write about how I see things from a historical perspective. Even though TV newsmakers and specialists have assessments, I have my own. The government has been working diligently to design a $2 trillion coronavirus stimulus package. President Trump is committed to getting some folk back to work by April 12. He said this Easter would go down in history, much like COVID-19, when we get through it.

Prayer: Heavenly Father, we are mourning people worldwide who are dying from the coronavirus. We pray for a cure while feeling fear, outrage, misery, confusion, panic, and hopelessness during this global suffering. As you test our faith, we trust you will arm us with the patience to endure this pandemic. Amen. March 2020.

Journaling with Media Messages about COVID-19

I intend to encourage you to write in your journal to get through each day despite the media painting a challenging canvas.

To those working from home, address incomplete projects on your PC, write letters, review unread proposals, and drum up businesses that can create funds post COVID-19. Finally, finish the various incomplete to-do lists tucked away. After you complete your work and have family time, you can write the poetry you've been working on in your psyche, compose that tune that stirs you every day, shift your resting artistic abilities, phone your loved ones who haven't heard your voice in some time, and read one good book. Create your list. We now have more time to do everything we've been putting off.

I sent my friend in California a request to help me with a book tour in 2021. As an independent contractor, he is frazzled because California received the stay-at-home mandate three days ago and he is still in denial, scratching his head, trying to figure out what to do. We're two weeks ahead with the governor's order in my state. So I'm settled in and working from home.

The benefit of writing about this period is communicating your feelings and developing a strategy for life's interferences. Your money and your movement are in question. Via TV, we're seeing our governors advise their state's residents to shelter in place and stay at home. Via the media, the federal government says that some may get cash to help stem setbacks. Our government is directing our money and movement. My information connections come through television and websites.

The media presents five big pictures: first, the White House report; second, the status of the pandemic; third, adversarial remarks about the White House report; fourth, Capitol Hill's exercises; and fifth, expert assessments.

Since the experts work from home, the interviews are via webcam. In addition to their personal opinions, we see how they live. We see their bookshelves, colorful painted and papered walls, ideal room settings, basement wood-paneled family rooms with paraphernalia, and the one blank wall for background. They are all in well-kept environments and likely will not receive $1200 from the government.

We feel their emotions because the experts speak from their homes' comfort with no scripts. They express their thoughts and expert conclusions with no staff assistance for fact-checking. If they're against Trump, he gets no praise, only slamming. On the off chance they're against Capitol Hill, then it gets no credit.

The TV media personalities interview only people who represent their way of thinking. They discuss what they already agree on, whether an expert or an ordinary citizen. Few disagreements show up in the media. They search to locate the right spokesperson to represent their supposition. Using that strategy, they don't appear as know-it-alls.

I attempt to watch various commentators to hear varying thoughts. However, there are more categorical likenesses than differences.

I want to write about how I see things for my history book. Even though the media, through newspapers, magazines, online reports, television interviewers and interviewees, and specialists are my sources, I should write my perspective on this coronavirus virus season. I should limit my access to news and data during this coronavirus season. I check in around noon to learn the media's plan for the day, around 6 p.m. for a preview of what's happening and approximately 11 p.m. for a synopsis of the day's events. Three times per day are too often because they say much of the same all day. In that event, I will attempt to hold off until eleven to give more time to the news and information I create for myself and the people close to me.

If you don't have a journal, find some writing paper and date each entry to keep it in order and make it your journal.

Prayer: Heavenly Father, we are overwhelmed by the myriad sources of information about COVID-19 that get through the media. We pray for our government to move quickly with the information for the public that it presents to the press. Our faith trusts that you will show us something new that we have never seen before to quell this coronavirus. Strengthen our faith. Thank you for guiding us to share comforting thoughts with others to help us overcome this pandemic. Amen. March 2020.

Journaling with Others in Mind During COVID-19

This section urges you to write in your journal to memorialize this season by adding this new dimension of transcribing to calm your spirit.

On Wednesday, one of my friends in New Jersey requested prayer for her godfather in a hospital emergency room with coronavirus symptoms. His sister-in-law tested positive on Friday. After the interaction, everybody got it. The godfather improved without coronavirus test results; however, doctors discovered pneumonia. On Friday, the godfather's oxygen levels were low, and doctors put him on a ventilator in the Intensive Care Unit (ICU). On Saturday, doctors removed the ventilator and pushed him out of the ICU. The rest of the relatives in the same house's tests were negative.

We know a story outside what we find in the media. As we mourn the deaths, we must pray continually for sick people—minute by minute, the number of cases and fatalities increases worldwide.

Unfortunately, we can do nothing to help the mourning families. However, we can connect with those who are presumed to be well. I phone, text, or email three individuals, one from my church roster, a family member, and a friend. Of course, I appreciate hearing from those who reach out to me.

I am writing about these conversations and comments in my journal, which add to my daily social communication. It's fascinating to learn how those with whom we are familiar are investing their energy nowadays.

Today, I got a request from a friend to participate in a Zoom to hang out on the web. Sounds interesting, so I purchased a web camera. After seeing the television experts telecommute from home with their cameras on their PCs, I am eager to try out this novel form of communication. My last blog limited my access to news and data during this coronavirus season. I check three times per day and may reduce it to two as information becomes increasingly redundant, with only changes in the cases and deaths.

You benefit from journaling about this coronavirus season by communicating your feelings in writing and creating new strategies for overcoming each day.

Prayer: Heavenly Father, we continue to mourn the deaths of people close and those from a distance. We pray that you are assisting the researchers with data to produce a cure for COVID-19. Our faith is trusting in you and leaning not on our understanding. We ask you to strengthen our faith. Thank you for guiding us to stay in touch with others and offering comforting thoughts. Amen. March 2020.

Journaling While We Mourn

This section recommends that you write in your journal to remember this coronavirus season by documenting mind-boggling events.

Approximately six weeks ago, my brother had a stroke at age fifty-one and became blind. He was in poor health, yet very upbeat and full of emotional passion for sharing with everyone around him. For the second time, he has had stents placed in his heart to help keep his coronary arteries open and decrease the chance of cardiac failure. At some point, he was on a feeding tube and a ventilator. When his blood pressure kept going down, they resurrected him. After the second resuscitation, his wife produced his living will, which denounced such action. He passed away at three in the morning, all alone.

Because his wife could not go inside the hospital, she regularly called the nearby nursing station. When he was transitioning from life to death, she used her mobile phone to whisper her parting words of love into his ears through a telephone in his intensive care unit space. Accordingly, we will wait until COVID-19 passes and have a memorial to celebrate his life.

To forestall the spread of COVID-19, hospitals have new regulations. If you're sick, call your primary care doctor. Change your in-person appointments to telephone calls. Hospitals are not allowing visitors or individuals who do not have a valid reason inside the doors. If you get inside, they look for symptoms identified with COVID-19. Furthermore, no recent international travelers are welcome.

Even though new guidelines intend to reduce the spread of the disease, employees stroll around the hospitals with neither masks nor gloves. Signs say to follow respiratory etiquette. I say stay away from hospitals if you can.

As we grieve a passing, we must pray continually for individuals who test positive and do not recuperate. Minute by minute, the number of cases and deaths increases worldwide.

The shelter-in-place and stay-at-home orders make it difficult for our relatives to grieve together. So we resort to lamenting using FaceTime via telephone. Such activity generally occurs while we travel and prepare for the funeral services. The government decrees no gatherings of more than ten.

I am attempting to describe that it is difficult to mourn alone in my journal. We have no arrangements to make, no food to prepare for visiting mourners, no gatherings to reminisce, no chuckling at photographs, and no need to take off bereavement days as we're staying at home and telecommuting.

I am sorry that my brother spent his last days in the hospital alone with no one at his bedside. I am sorry I could not travel one hundred miles to comfort my sister and his wife. I am sorry that hospice was not there to support our family and friends during his final days. I am sorry hospice was not there to focus on making him comfortable and helping him smile. He was such a pleasant kind of guy.

You can read my pitifulness. Writing in my journal helps me get through my sorrow and permits me to write and write and write about my sibling. I will benefit from journaling this season. Despite his sicknesses, he tested positive for COVID-19.

Prayer: Heavenly Father, my heart feels wounded, and my mind is sorrowful like many others; as we mourn the deaths of people we love and others, we notice. We pray that you give us the strength to persevere with deaths during this heartbreaking time of COVID-19. Help us to be hopeful while we learn of increasing deaths. Please fortify our faith while these happenings eat at our souls. Thank you for being our hospice. Amen. March 2020.

Journaling and Being Creative during COVID-19

The governor's shelter-in-place and stay-at-home requests make it difficult for family members to grieve together. Accordingly, we will wait until we can assemble again after COVID-19 passes to have memorials to commend the lives of our family and friends. Perhaps, we should have a National Day of Prayer and Remembrance for COVID-19. President Bush proclaimed such a day on Friday, September 14, 2001, for the victims of the terrorist attacks on September 11, 2001.

In addition to writing a blog, I am the author of *Journal It! Take Hold of Your Life by Journaling*, two holy books, and a book of poetry, *Feeling Wheels*. I love my book of poetry since it has 250 poems and songs that mirror my emotions on any given day. When I reread pages, they help me remember where I was.

This freedom of time and constrained space is an ideal opportunity to be imaginative. I'm composing quatrains, poems with four lines. Mine have varying forms and meters, and every one portrays a feeling. Many writers wrote mainstream pandemic poems.

As an advocate of journaling, I realize that words are incredible, provoking, powerful, and healing. Writing can enable us to describe what we feel and see to remind us that this coronavirus season will pass. Journaling can help us come to grips with the upheaval of our lives. We can utilize our talents, gifts, and dreams to create expressions. We can be reminders of what the world is now and envision what's to come.

I see numerous essays and poems that reflect some aspects of this coronavirus season. As a writer, I read what individuals are composing. Notwithstanding, if I were an artist, I would draw a picture of my mind. If I were a songwriter, I would compose a memorial song. If I were a storyteller, I would write a story. If I were a novelist, I would pen a novel. If I were a historian, I would document all that is happening.

The fine art of persuasion or creative visual artistry produces outstanding, imaginative, and scholarly substance. Your artistic skill and innovative minds, such as painting or sculpture, visually work for beauty or emotional power. Now is undoubtedly the time to retrieve that draft play or script for the movie or documentary you need to create. Perhaps, your creation will be a memorable piece of the "art of COVID-19."

Art, like love, knows no bounds yet opens up new expressions and pictures that reassure us there will be a wonderful new day tomorrow if we stay together and hold on and see the beauty in these critical times.

In my journal, I stay away from negativity or criticism. I am prayerful as I use scriptures to compose prayers. My books *The Prayor: One Who Prays* and *The Prayor Worships with Isaiah* have Bible verses and prayers. Here are my scriptures and prayer for this day:

"The steadfast love of the Lord never ceases; his mercies never come to an end; they are new every morning; great is your faithfulness" (Lam 3:22–23). "But they who wait for the Lord shall renew their strength; they shall mount up with wings like eagles; they shall run and not be weary; they shall walk and not faint" (Isa 40:31).

Prayer: Heavenly Father, this COVID-19 season has changed how we go through our days. Some of us have an expanse of time to think and create without end. Help us use our abilities to appreciate our artistic expressions when this pandemic ends, as I trust it will end. Please direct us to use our time by renewing our strength to prevail by using the talents you gave us. Thank you for loving us. Amen. March 2020.

Journaling on Holy Thursday

Today is Holy Thursday or Maundy Thursday, unquestionably a day of remembrances.

During Holy Week, we ponder on a historical tradition. Christians throughout the world are observing Holy Thursday or Maundy Thursday. Maundy originates from the Latin word mando, which means to order or command. For Holy Week, it alludes to the commandment Jesus provided for his disciples to finish his final act of service for his disciples. He stated, "I have set you an example that you should do as I have done for you" (John 13:15).

Further, he says explicitly, "A new command I give you: Love one another. As I have loved you, so you must love one another. By this, everyone will know that you are my disciples if you love one another" (John 13:34–35).

This Holy Week is unique, as is Maundy Thursday. Christians have been praying for weeks since the coming of the pandemic. We are saying we believe God is still in charge, yet, COVID-19 tests our faith. I do not want the coronavirus to saturate every paragraph of my outline of praise, thanksgiving, and requests in my prayer journal. Even though we have stay-at-home orders, this all-consuming plague mandates how we live.

There are plagues referenced in the Bible. I will not join the individuals who liken the coronavirus pandemic to the plague, which the Bible mentions by the prophet John in Revelation. Food shortages, fear, viruses, and economic collapse anticipate the end times. Like other plagues in the Bible and history, this pandemic will pass, and after we grieve the losses of our loved ones, money, businesses, and property, we will think back, read our journals, and recall how lives can change in a couple of months.

Since Lent started and news of the pandemic came daily, I find new prayer calls and sermons on my cellphone or the web. I pray continually with eleven other prayer warriors. On each call, there are new prayer requests. With the spread of COVID-19, more individuals request prayer. We submit names and monitor their progress to express our explicit gratitude to God. There is never a time when we have no petitions. Be that as it may, this Holy Week humbles us and helps us remember Jesus' command to love and serve one another.

The media analyzes words, statistics, and studies that follow COVID-19. However, reporters daily infuse something about this Holy Week. Its sheer repetitious acknowledgment has been astounding. Some say Easter will send us back to our work environments and restaurants and shopping centers will reopen. That may not be so, yet Easter has gotten more airtime than I can recall. Even in my meditative journal, I have more scriptures focusing on trusting God and not on my understanding during this Holy Week.

On Maundy Thursday, Jesus advised his disciples to love one another and serve people. He knew something unprecedented was happening. Your journal imperative is to expound on the amazing things that happen every day and remember that we got through the pandemic with slimmer bodies, changed lives, pulled together personalities, and hearts of gold.

Prayer: Heavenly Father, these holy weekdays between Palm Sunday and Easter give us a particular time to recollect the Passion of Jesus Christ and recall your incredible deeds. It is generally a period of celebration given your resurrection on Easter Sunday. COVID-19 makes it a time filled with sadness and hopelessness. But, in you, there is light. There is no darkness. Help us to celebrate and remember your holiness during this Holy Week. Amen. April 2020.

Journaling after Easter

This year's Easter Sunday did not require new hats and spring outfits because we sat at home or in our vehicles to watch or tune in to accept the passion of Christ. Without a doubt, it felt different, but the messages were the same. We should journal about the newness of this celebration.

After Maundy Thursday, Easter weekend begins on Good Friday, Christ's crucifixion; Saturday or Easter Eve, when Christ lay in his tomb; and Easter Sunday, Christ's resurrection. Sunday is our day of rejoicing and rebirth that carries eternal life to his followers.

In my church, we fast and eat no meat on Friday. We pray in all-night vigils on Saturday. Sunday begins with a sunrise service. Later, during Sunday Service, the school-age youth present contemporary theater, song, and dance to celebrate our risen Savior. Following Service, families join together for Easter meals, egg decorating, and baskets for the children. With the coronavirus around us, we chose to celebrate it differently.

The media promotes social distancing and stay-at-home orders while challenging church leaders to figure out something that does not require them to assemble inside church buildings.

Governors' stay-at-home orders to constrain the spread of COVID-19 require different ways to spend Easter weekend. Social distancing eliminates Sunday church service in the sanctuaries. Easter brunch is not available in a restaurant, just takeout.

Church leaders create new ways to communicate their sermons and songs. Group phone-ins via FreeConferenceCall.com are especially easy for the elderly who don't have online access. The likes of Zoom and WebEx help to see everyone on PCs or smart phones. Beyond technology, churches are replicating drive-in theaters in their parking lots with the speaker and musicians on a stage or the church steps standing six feet apart.

We listened to our minister on our smart phones. We viewed an Easter-oriented play and two sermons on TV and the Bible marathon on the History Channel. We will stay in the Holy Week frame of mind throughout the week by watching *Jesus Christ Superstar* and some of the best Easter movies ever made.

Our journal describes how this Easter weekend differs from those in our past lives. We explain how we celebrate at home or in our cars with no new Easter bonnet or outfit due to the coronavirus.

Prayer: Heavenly Father, you loved the world and gave your only son to have eternal life. We celebrate the resurrection of Jesus Christ at Easter in new ways because of COVID-19. We miss being near church members and embracing our friends and family. Help us celebrate in our hearts and minds while remembering your holiness. Thank you for guiding us to different ways to acknowledge you. Amen. April 2020.

Journaling While Shifting Gears

Easter has passed, and now we wait for Ascension Thursday, May 21, 2020, forty days after Easter, when Jesus ascended to heaven. While we wait to celebrate, we shift our life gears to a new normal. By May 21, perhaps we will begin venturing outside the governors' stay-at-home orders and gathering in small public groups. Until then, we journal to rev up our engines.

Perhaps we can shorten our social distance to closer than six feet. Matching masks and colorful plastic gloves are additions to our wardrobes. Part of our health safety may be regular testing prescribed by every physician who sees patients. If testing positive, fourteen days for quarantine will be doable and acceptable. I want to request a COVID-19 test within the next forty days to allow plenty of time for quarantine, should it be necessary.

As I journal to prepare for Ascension Thursday, I will write about what I want to accomplish. During Lent, I had a to-do list of thirty-six things to do. Although I worked on them, I did not complete one item. Of course, I blame my incapacity on the interruption of the coronavirus. It impacts my spirit, mind, and ability to focus.

In my "writing forward" journal, which includes the desires of my heart, I dream of life after COVID-19. Although there will be a new normal, I hope to take a winter and summer vacation in 2022. I plan to add some memories of past travels and what makes them most memorable. Replicating some adventures and searching the travelogues will help create new dreams.

Now that I am officially sheltering in place at home, my new list for the next forty days has only thirty things to do. Most importantly, I plan to start a new novel and develop my blog further.

National leaders are addressing significant issues impacting many lives during this season. What shall we do? The baseball season is about to begin. We should sequester all the teams and their families in a community of approximately 20,000 with clinics and libraries, where thirty teams can play 162 baseball games. Doctors and care providers can take daily temperatures and periodic tests to ensure they remain healthy. Organizations, their families, and caregivers may serve as the live audience. The rest of us can watch it on TV.

Further, this experiment will allow enough time for other sports to figure out their strategies for play. The media promotes social distancing and stay-at-home orders. The nationwide plan is to reopen gradually with companies that can practice social distancing, cleaning protocols, and other measures to reduce the spread of the coronavirus.

Our journals should describe this coronavirus season as one of our drives through life when we shift gears by working from home, creating new work, having no job, relaxing, and restructuring our lives. This season compares with no other in our past, yet we must ready ourselves for a new normal with fresh dreams and adventures, all due to the coronavirus.

"For I am about to do something new. See, I have already begun! Do you not see it? I will make a pathway through the wilderness. I will create rivers in the dry wasteland" (Isa 43:19).

Prayer: Heavenly Father, we praise you for our risen savior. We know you have our lives in your hands. We trust that you will restore us to your chosen people. Thank you for enlarging our territories during this COVID season. Dear God, we're glad to give you praise. Amen. April 2020.

Journaling about COVID-19 Money

The Coronavirus Aid, Relief, and Economic Security Act, known as the CARES Act or the $2 Trillion COVID-19 Stimulus Bill, is traversing the country. The money goes through central banks, big and small businesses, state and local governments, and directly to individuals like you and me. Since the cash is on its way, we should quickly decide how to spend a newly won lottery and stimulate our financial agendas.

According to the Stimulus Bill, $603.7 billion will go towards cash payments to individuals and families. It will be a $1,200 payment for those earning up to $75,000 a year. Cash sums phase out for higher earners, ending at the $99,000 income level. Families will also receive $500 per child.

Big businesses gain $500 billion to stabilize hard-hit sectors, for example, the airline industry. Small businesses get $377 billion through the Small Business Administration (SBA) to provide loans for qualifying organizations and grants for companies that need assistance covering short-term operating expenses.

State and Local Governments' portions total $340 billion for direct COVID-19 issues and schools and childcare services.

Public and Health Services receive $179.5 million in grants to help battle COVID-19. There will also be a twenty percent increase in Medicare installments for treating patients with the coronavirus.

Money is also set aside for initiatives such as increasing the availability of ventilators and masks for the Strategic National Stockpile and providing additional funding for additional staffing for the CDC.

Finally, beyond the healthcare-related funding, the CARES Act also addresses food, security projects, educational programs, and arts initiatives.

What you want your financial position to be is most important. Before going through any money, make a plan that incorporates critical cash needs. Credit card companies and mortgage companies are willing to make deals that include postponing installments. We should make a budget that extends through the last check and focuses on buying time and saving money for unemployment payments.

So what shall we write about our newly-found funds? Make another segment in our coronavirus journal for COVID-19 money. I suggest handling the emergent needs, creating emergency fund savings, and sitting tight until the next money crisis. We don't know whether we will get more cash from the government. Having some spare change or an unexpected cash cushion will be helpful.

Since we stay at home with no place to go, our spending requirements are minimal. Online shopping is a no-no.

"Therefore, do not worry about tomorrow, for tomorrow will worry itself. Each day has enough trouble of its own" (Matt 6:34).

Prayer: Heavenly Father, as we sit and wait for funding from the government, help us give our best to you and follow your lead. Guide us to spend the money wisely and share some with at least one person. We trust that you will meet all our needs according to the riches of your glory in Christ Jesus. Thank you. Amen. April 2020.

Journaling about Our Share of $2 Trillion

Some businesses, local governments, and individuals are now receiving their funds. Regretfully, mine is not yet in my bank.

The IRS and other money-related communicators have online instructions that disclose how to get the status of payments. Below is information from the irs.gov website under "Get My Payment" about the economic impact payments (EIP):

> Get My Payment provides one of two statuses. 1. Process a payment, avail the payment date, and indicate the payment's transmittal by direct deposit or mail. 2. You are eligible, but payment has not been processed, and the payment date is unavailable.
>
> If you are eligible for a payment, but IRS does not have your direct deposit information. You will be allowed to provide your bank information once you have correctly verified your identity. Direct Deposit is the fastest way to get your EIP.
>
> IRS cannot determine your eligibility for payment at this time. For example, you didn't file either a 2018 or 2019 tax return or recently filed one, and the return has not been fully processed.
>
> If a payment date is not provided, updates to your payment status are made no more than once a day.[2]

2. https://www.irs.gov/newsroom/heres-how-to-get-the-status-of-an-economic-impact-payment

I must be patient because our government says more than eighty percent of Americans will receive funds. Congress declares it will take five months to issue all the payments. My EIP plan is to purchase two small items and use the balance to make an emergency fund savings and sit tight until the next money crisis. Since I'm staying at home with no place to go, my necessities are minimal.

"Keep your lives free from the love of money and be content with what you have because God has said 'Never will I leave you; never will I forsake you'" (Heb 13:5).

Prayer: Heavenly Father, COVID-19 has disrupted our lives in many ways and interrupted how we spend and acquire money. We have confidence that your favor brings wealth, and we must honor you first. Guide us to pay those we owe as we will rejoice in following your lead. We accept that everything comes from you. Thank you for these forthcoming blessings. Amen. April 2020.

Journaling Staying In vs. Going Out

Commands such as stay at home, close your business, take part in virtual classes, and shelter in place are unfathomable, coming from our local and national government leaders. However, COVID-19, a new human infectious disease, fuels new ideas in our daily lives. Staying in or going out seems to be a simple concept to follow, but one of necessity.

The White House Coronavirus Task Force wants Americans to move slowly toward re-openings in the coming months and keep social distancing measures throughout the summer.

Testing is the barometer to get a more accurate picture of the coronavirus spreading. The diagnostic testing tests an individual's nose or mouth fluid sample for evidence of a live coronavirus.

Scientists and doctors express dissatisfaction that a few states are moving too fast to return to some economic normalcy. Protestors are requesting that businesses open up now. They want employees back to work because companies continue to feel the monetary strain.

Our governor in Ohio plans to begin with gradual openings on May 1. Facial coverings will be necessary for all customers and employees inside businesses. His guidelines are comparable to the safety rules that OSHA and FDA demand. The reopening will start with companies creating a safe environment that accentuates safety for employees and customers. Health care procedures and dental and veterinarian services may open on May 1. Elective surgeries may resume on March 17. Manufacturing, distribution, and construction companies could reopen on May 4. Organizations that operate in office settings should plan to open on May 4. Consumer services and retail stores might reopen on May 12.

There's no date for eat-in restaurants, bars, beauty businesses, adult daycare services, senior centers, and casinos. Parents eagerly await daycare services for children, recreation centers, swimming pools, summer camps, theme parks, and playgrounds.

I wear a mask and gloves to protect myself and others whenever I venture away. Now I pick up my groceries curbside and only go inside the drug store. Both errands comprise my total weekly outings. However, I don't know when I will feel comfortable going to my nail salon or strolling around shopping venues. I need to journal my plans.

Since we're sheltering in place and staying at home, we miss some places and things. It's an ideal opportunity to set up another section in our journals. I will list the locations I miss in my journal and describe why I am eager to return. When to return is the real question. I intend to start with a comfortable walk in the park to see what's happening. I will drive around town and check out the open businesses. I will write a strategy for my upcoming home journeys in my journal.

"Do not conform to the pattern of this world, but be transformed by the renewing of your mind. Then you will be able to test and approve what God's will is—his good, pleasing, and perfect will" (Rom 12:2).

Prayer: Heavenly Father, after staying at home and limiting my socialization with others, I am starting to think about going out and about. Help me comprehend the depth of change that

COVID-19 makes in the world. Guide me to your will for reestablishing my life in this coronavirus season. I believe you will make firm the steps you built for us to climb. Thank you for your perfect will. Amen. May 2020.

Journaling about Coronavirus Masks

Hi-ho, hi-ho silver! Here comes the Lone Ranger to the rescue. This masked ranger hides his identity, fighting for law and order. He fashions a black mask using cloth from his late brother's vest. When he leaves at the show's end, somebody always asks, "Who was that masked man?" The answer is, "That was the Lone Ranger." Can you imagine how this world will be like a movie when we all don masks in public?

Like the Lone Ranger, we will be battling the coronavirus to guard ourselves and others who may say, "Who was that masked person?" As our face coverings tell them, they will know, "We're the exceptional folk fighting to kill COVID-19."

As states regulate the businesses' right to open, the governors must say when. In addition to following government practices that oversee risks of spreading COVID-19, such as social distancing and protective equipment, we will wear face masks. The CDC recommends wearing cloth face coverings in public settings and avoiding areas where individuals sit and stand close together. Don't be surprised if a business employee asks to check your bags and temperature before entering their space. What's more, the manager may make the request that you leave. Some infected people can transmit the coronavirus even without displaying symptoms. However, a temperature check is a close look at whether your body is putting out more or less heat than usual. If so, it's letting you know there's an issue.

Medical specialists tell us wearing a mask slows the spread of the disease. COVID-19 can spread among people nearby — for instance, speaking, coughing, or sneezing — regardless of whether those individuals display symptoms. The Lone Ranger wore his mask to conceal his identity as he was the sole survivor of a group of rangers killed in an ambush. His mission was to fight for law and order. We should wear face masks to cover our nose and mouth to block the release of virus-filled drops into the air when coughing or sneezing. The main benefit is to protect the people around you and keep law and order.

Try not to rush out and purchase a mask; leave the N-95s and other surgical masks for health care providers who urgently need them. The web offers advice and directions on making a face covering at home. If you google "coronavirus mask," you can find 1,380,000,000 results.

During World War I, historical events created fashion items out of necessity, such as pants for women. Casual sportswear is the standard as we work from home, in cubicles at offices, and dress in jeans on Fridays. A simple dress is becoming the norm, except when wearing a uniform. We add masks to our wardrobes as a necessary accessory that goes out with us.

The mask is now part of our fashion accessories that enhance our outfits. We will pay special attention to them and select just as carefully as we do our jewelry, handbags, scarves, hats, belts, ties, leggings, socks, hair accessories, umbrellas, boots, and gloves. I have eight masks: four blue and white ones that I got from the hospital, along with four handmade ones, two blue and white checks, one navy print, and one red print.

Now I need to add in-vogue face coverings to my wardrobe. I discovered eighteen-inch scarves in my scarf box that will make gorgeous masks. Also, I found various scarves I haven't worn in some time. They are ready for reuse and cutting. Besides, I've got some long dresses and skirts that I can cut off to make matching scarves. If I can't shop enough in my closet, Amazon shows 719 coronaviruses face masks.

I must take photographs of my face coverings and place them in my coronavirus journal. I pray that COVID-19 fashion passes similarly to Nehru jackets and bell-bottom pants. I want my granddaughter to see the natural history of the coronavirus pandemic in 2020.

"Therefore I tell you, do not worry about your life, what you will eat or drink; or about your body, what you will wear. Is not life more than food and the body more than clothes?" (Matt 6:25).

Prayer: Heavenly Father, we are being asked to wear face coverings to avoid passing the coronavirus. Masks are uncomfortable for a while as they are hot and require speaking loudly and clearly. Help us not worry about this requirement and treat it as a necessity. Guide us as we make life changes during this coronavirus season. We believe you have given us more fulfilling lives than the clothing we adorn our bodies. Thank you. Amen. May 2020.

Journaling about Mother's Day and COVID-19

Mother's Day is fabulous for taking Mother to brunch or dinner. Not so in 2020. Many restaurants are promoting their menus at reasonable costs for takeout only. You appear to save money on missing the ambiance. No state has opened dine-in eateries during this coronavirus season. What shall we do for Mother?

Mother's Day requires that we become creative if Mother is nearby. Don your mask and go for takeout food and drink. Or purchase a gift. Curbside service delivery is available for kitchen and cooking equipment, bath and beauty products, flowers, and unique items from specialty stores. Call ahead and your Mother's Day gift will be waiting.

FaceTime, Zoom, Skype, and WebEx are perfect for mothers and grandmothers who live far away. Mother's Day is a great chance to teach everybody to use these video communications tools. With your Smartphone, you can talk to and see many people on video chat. With an Android or PC, you can see more clearly.

Even though I am the mother, we will dine at our son-in-law's and daughter's home. We will celebrate her first Mother's Day with their twelve-week-old baby girl. There will be just six of us and the infant. Of course, we will wear face coverings when holding her and keep a social distance during our visit. Above all, remember this coronavirus season is temporary. COVID-19 will pass.

"But watch out! Be very careful never to forget what you have seen God doing for you. May his miracles have a serious and permanent effect on your lives! Tell your children and grandchildren about the glorious miracles he did" (Deut 4:9).

Prayer: Heavenly Father, we celebrate our mothers and respect them properly, whether they yet live. On this day, we will not have the option to celebrate as we usually do by eating in restaurants and traveling cross country. Help us be mindful of these times and keep memorabilia from this coronavirus season. Guide us as we speak of you and detail the miracles we have seen and our endured times. Thank you for allowing us to have children and grandchildren with whom we can share your works. Amen. May 2020.

Journaling after Mother's Day during COVID-19

We overcame Mother's Day with little stress and lots of joy. We gathered at our son-in-law's and daughter's home to celebrate her and me as mothers. There were only six of us, including the baby girl. We didn't wear face covers, yet we practiced social distancing. We ate buffet-style food to fill our plates and find a spot away from the table to dine. It was a most enjoyable day.

Before Mother's Day, as I rode around town, I saw barely anyone wearing material face covers in public settings. They only wore them inside businesses with signs saying: "No one can enter without a face covering." Stay-at-home or shelter-in-place orders across the country are decreasing in some states, and others are extending the days during the coronavirus pandemic season.

I saw children with signs and balloons expressing adoration in grandmas' yards. Many children were doing yard work with Happy Mother's Day signs. One vehicle full of people held signs outside the windows saying "Happy Mother's Day." Youngsters played musical instruments in yards with signs saying "Happy Mother's Day."

When I checked in with my friends, many had food delivered from their favorite restaurants. Video gatherings included fixing dinner and eating together, games, cocktail parties, talent shows, art exhibits, and talking about a movie.

We got through this Mother's Day using ways to make it memorable. One year, we ought to move about and travel more efficiently. We can become progressively more creative with our Mother's Day festivities after COVID-19 passes. How about now we look at what's to come?

"No, dear brothers and sisters, I have not achieved it, but I focus on this one thing: Forgetting the past and looking forward to what lies ahead, I press on to reach the end of the race and receive the heavenly prize for which God, through Christ Jesus, is calling us" (Phil 3:13–14).

Prayer: Heavenly Father, we continue to respect our mothers. On Mother's Day, we celebrated in ways unlike our past dining habits in restaurants and traveling cross country. Please help us to focus on looking forward to what lies ahead. Our encounters during COVID-19 make us press toward when this virus season ends. Give us comfort as we encourage others toward the future with a new normal that is acceptable to your calling. Thank you for the opportunity to believe another great year is ahead. Amen. May 2020.

Journaling in COVID-19—Wear Masks and Face Covers

Across the country, people are pushing through the coronavirus storm and learning how to dance in the rain by returning to work, dining inside and outside restaurants, shopping in partially opened shopping centers, and moving about outside. We celebrated Mother's Day with little trouble and lots of joy. Now we're prepared for genuine journeys. However, the issues that face us collectively mandate wearing masks and social distancing.

Face coverings of any kind serve as protective gear. Masks don't offer complete protection from the coronavirus. However, experts report that wearing a mask ensures less transmission by virus carriers. Data show that one in four people infected with COVID-19 is asymptomatic and unaware of their contamination.

Ohio's governor insisted that Ohioans wear face covers inside stores. Then he changed the order in light of so much rapid opposition. He adjusted his perspective within twenty-four hours. The mask protesters won their freedom to decide how they remain safe, to the detriment of others. I accept they're overlooking the central issue of wearing a mask. The advantage of wearing a face cover is to protect the individuals around you. Coronavirus transmits from people without symptoms to new bodies. A mask prevents germs from coughing, wheezing, breathing, and transferring infection. Wearing a mask lessens the probability of individuals spreading the sickness.

One study shows that if eighty percent of the population wears masks, forty-five percent of projected deaths will lessen over the next two months. Today, there are 4.5 million coronavirus cases globally, and 1.4 million in the US. Deaths total 306,050 around the globe and 86,850 in the US. The magnitude of those numbers gives us cause to wear masks to protect people close to us as we move about and return to life's everyday journeys.

The US health authorities updated guidelines for reopening schools, businesses, and other people-centered organizations. The specifics still include wearing masks and spacing workers or students six feet apart and wearing masks. Health experts say cloth coverings will help stop the spread of the coronavirus that has affected more than 6.5 million around the globe of more than 7 billion inhabitants.

"Blessed is the one whose transgressions are forgiven, and whose sins are covered" (Ps 32:1).

Prayer: Heavenly Father, we are asked to cover our faces with masks to not hurt others by merely breathing into their faces. Help us to understand that we will not forgive ourselves if we hurt others. Please forgive us our trespasses as we forgive those who trespass against us. Please give us a sense of comfort as we cover the spreading of the coronavirus. Thank you for the opportunity to help one another. Amen. May 2020.

Journaling the Journey Outside, Post-Stay-at-Home

Businesses are beginning to reopen as the coronavirus subsides. I went out and was about to eyeball things and saw a limited number of facial covers and no plastic gloves. There are gates and signs on shop floors to demonstrate where to stand and stay 6 feet apart. Restaurants look different with unique seating arrangements, disposable menus, and table dividers. Plexiglas separations are everywhere to protect the clerks in drug stores, groceries, markets, and retail establishments.

I saw many people congregating in the parks and open spaces. Social distancing and mask-wearing are not the norm. It appears as though people believe that being outside permits you to breathe and converse with no face coverings, even though coronavirus continues to spread. Most groups I saw totaled less than ten and were roughly six feet away from nearby gatherings.

There are no beaches near my community, but many people stroll along the riverside, generally couples and parents with children. Few are wearing masks, but many are running and walking while appreciating the freedom of open space after staying home.

The government's national guidelines incorporate testing sites for symptomatic individuals, tracing contacts of COVID-19 results, and surveillance sites for screening asymptomatic folks. The rules also require that healthcare systems be ready and able to deal with the community's needs. The ultimate plan is to ensure the well-being and safety of workers and their clientele, whether in a closed space or mass transit. Finally, the local government leaders must monitor the conditions and advise citizens regarding necessary mandates to keep everyone safe.

"Not looking to your own interests but each of you to the interests of the others" (Phil 2:4).

Prayer: Heavenly Father, as we move away from sheltering and venture outside our homes, we must think of others and ourselves. Please help us understand the need to believe that we must respect the same safety of others as we want for ourselves. Be patient as we comply with the safety guidelines when entering establishments with employees and other customers. Please help us to consider the interests of others during this coronavirus season. Thank you for the opportunity to help one another. Amen. June 2020.

Journaling the Protests

Since it may take years to discover a cure and a vaccine, many individuals contract the coronavirus. Nevertheless, millions of people protest in large gatherings, and few wear face coverings. There is no telling what new COVID-19 statistics will divulge over five to seven days.

Numerous individuals are returning to the streets and protesting about the recent attacks by police on African Americans, specifically Breonna Taylor in Louisville, Kentucky, and George Floyd in Minneapolis, whose death we witnessed via camcorders. His death provoked a call to action by protesting leaders around the world. In more than four hundred cities and dozens of foreign counties, people have taken to the streets to express their support for Black Lives Matter. People who are black, white, brown, and Asian are marching with their parents, children, and grandchildren to show their support. The LGBTQ folk are in the crowds as they often feel the brunt of over-zealous police officers. Demonstrators gather in large and small groups, screaming chants demanding justice. Regardless of the purpose of the protests, police continue to use their heavy hands of force. What now? We won't go back to our regular routines of getting up early to have breakfast with our children and getting them off to daycare and school before going to work. There is no job, daycare has not reopened, and school is on summer break. This situation directly results from the pandemic, not police brutality or protests. However, the pandemic and protests will both command change. The world is waiting for a cure and vaccines for COVID-19.

What's more, the sentiment of the protestors is to invoke police reform and create something new. It may not be the old normal. The risk of spreading COVID-19 is confusing when a cause addresses racial inequities that include black people dying at almost twice their proportion of the population. Now scientists must reconsider how coronavirus spreads during numerous gatherings and few masks. People are willing to risk their lives, as risky as it is for people to spread and contract the coronavirus. We pray the virus germs will disappear in the sunny, humid outdoors.

My book *Journal It! Take Hold of Your Life by Journaling* lists fifty distinct approaches. News clippings and quotes from television and radio summarize unforgettable news and occasions that impact our lives. The combined demonstrations of the pandemic and the protests may be far too much for writing. If you're protesting, include photo journaling with your mobile phone to capture your surroundings and the people you're assembling or those more than 6 feet away. Create a separate album for protesting that includes outcomes that will be part of this saga. Now it is critical to write down what we've seen, believed, and heard.

"Their sins and lawless acts I will remember no more" (Heb 10:17).

Prayer: Heavenly Father, in recent months, the protestors and the police have been at odds in warfare created by unnecessary violent acts of force by police officers. Encompass an air of forgiveness around us that we might move forward. Guide our leaders to prepare a framework of law that fits all citizens. Thank you for not remembering and forgiving all our sins and lawless acts. Amen. June 2020.

Journaling about LGBTQ Supreme Court Law

During the pandemic, your journal records extraordinary events affecting the world. Our nation's work continues during this coronavirus season and civil rights protests. The Supreme Court remains in session even though some justices telecommute. The Supreme Court ruled on a milestone social equality law barring sex discrimination against gay, lesbian, and transgender workers in the work environment.

The LGBTQ community walks among the crowds while remembering their battle for social justice. The fatal shooting of a black transgender man in Tallahassee, Florida, recently sparked local protests. In contrast, mass protests and violence continue to erupt in cities worldwide following the death of George Floyd at the hands of police officers.

Outcries for human value, common equity, and civil justice have gone on since the 1800s. In 2003, the Court extended LGBTQ human rights by applying workplace protections for employees for the third time. The 1964 civil rights law text bars employment discrimination based on sex.

When Congress enacted civil rights legislation in 1964, the American Psychiatric Association deemed homosexuality a "psychiatric disorder," and many states criminalized gay behavior. With limited constitutional protections, members of the LGBTQ community faced discrimination and persecution.

Promulgated to protect African-Americans at the height of the civil rights movement, Title VII of the 1964 bill prohibited discrimination in the workplace based upon a person's "race, color, religion, sex, or national origin." Lawyers say that despite the acknowledgment of LGBTQ workers, most jurisdictions in the United States offer no employment protections for these individuals. The Supreme Court's decree protects LGBTQ people from discrimination in employment.

"I will be glad and rejoice in your love, for you saw my affliction and knew the anguish of my soul" (Ps 31:7).

Prayer: Heavenly Father, for years, the courts have wrestled with the pros and cons of civil and human rights granted to citizens of our country. We continue to protest for changes that include everyone. We are at odds with those who cause unfair practices in the workplace and violent acts of force by others. Fill the air with unrequited love for one another to move forward, treating everyone equally. Whatever pain we hold, calm that affliction and anguish of our souls. Please continue to help our leaders prepare a law framework that includes all citizens. Thank you for guiding the Supreme Court to eliminate further discrimination toward LGBTQ people. Amen. June 2020.

Journaling Civil Rights and Protests

History repeats itself—outcries for human value, common equity, and civil rights have gone on for more than 150 years. Civil rights speak to a specific set of rights designed to protect individuals from unjust actions and guarantee equal education, employment, and housing treatment. Now we must add equal treatment by police officers. Thus, everyone should be free from discrimination.

Alongside the Fourteenth and Fifteenth Amendments, the Thirteenth Amendment was the first of the three Reconstruction Period amendments adopted following the Civil War. The Emancipation Proclamation of 1863 freed slaves only in the eleven Confederate states.

In July 1866, Congress passed the first civil rights bill based upon its power under the Thirteenth and Fourteenth Amendments to enforce these rights guaranteeing citizenship, equal protection of the law, and due process to former slaves.

Two months before Congress passed the Civil Rights Bill, the 1866 Memphis massacre killed forty-six African Americans, and two white people died. White mobs, including police officers, firefighters, and businesspeople attacked the freedmen's camps and neighborhoods.

The Memphis race riot reflected the attitudes of most white citizens toward the former black slaves, who were then free and demanded equal rights. As a result of many such disturbances, leaders enacted laws to protect freedmen, who ultimately became citizens, voters, and government officeholders.

The most recent civil rights movement was an organized effort by African Americans to end racial discrimination and gain equal rights. It began in the late 1940s and ended in the late 1960s. Some gatherings were nonviolent but sometimes became violent. Such protests resulted in legislation to protect every American's constitutional civil rights. We return to a point in history now focusing on police officers' reform to protect individuals' constitutional civil rights, regardless of color, race, sex, or national origin. Today, people of all colors and types are protesting, marching, rioting, organizing, and dying for civil rights legislation. Congress is working on laws that will change how police officers conduct themselves. What we think of new laws related to police reform and how we handle ourselves should be noted in our journals as changes occur. "And if I do what I do not want to do, I agree that the law is good" (Rom 7:16).

Prayer: Heavenly Father, for years, Congress and the Supreme Court have written laws that grant civil and human rights to include all people of this nation. We continue to protest for changes that include everyone. People of all colors are protesting for fair treatment. Fill the air with unrequited love to move forward, treating everyone equally. Please help our Congress and leaders continue to prepare laws to benefit all citizens. Thank you for guiding legislatures to enact legislation that meets the needs of the people. Amen. June 2020.

Journaling 4th of July

Around the world, individuals have been communicating dissatisfaction with racial injustices for one hundred days. There have been protests in at least 1,750 locales in all fifty United States. The initial demonstrations started after the world viewed the police killing of George Floyd on TV on March 25, 2020. Protests continue developing day by day. Plans for demonstrations in more communities will build this Fourth of July weekend.

Consequently, events on the Fourth of July will celebrate and criticize, thereby reflecting on the problems and the promises of the nation's history and recent developments. Displays of fireworks, family gatherings, and protests will happen across the United States this Independence Day, a federal holiday recognizing the Declaration of Independence of the United States on July 4, 1776.

The first Fourth of July protest occurred after signing the Declaration in 1776. Some Philadelphians enjoyed fireworks and festivities as other pro-war Philadelphians committed acts of violence.

For the better part of the nineteenth century, many groups like abolitionists, African Americans, Native Americans, socialists, religious leaders, women's suffragists, and industrial workers gathered on the Fourth of July to express their concerns for social justice.

The annual tradition of July 4th marches declined in the twentieth century. Yet, it reappeared periodically to call attention to the Vietnam War, the "Black Declaration of Independence" grievances, Veterans Administration hospitals, Agent Orange, LGBTQ Rights, and the Affordable Care Act.

We shall see the aftereffects of prearranged protests and actions across the country. This Fourth of July weekend and other countries around the globe will probably join us. More than two thousand cities will continue to focus on racial injustices after the killing of George Floyd. The list includes many issues, such as naming specific persons killed by police officers, police reform, and the anxiety related to COVID-19. Then specific new ideas were added, such as wearing masks, business openings, removal of statues, racial symbols, LGBTQ pride, veterans' needs, getting out the vote, elections, Black Lives Matter, and "all lives matter."

"Truly, I tell you, wherever this gospel is preached throughout the world, what she has done will also be told, in memory of her" (Matt 26:13).

Prayer: Heavenly Father, we want to remember COVID-19 as a life-changing narrative we witnessed in our lifetime. Help us write our perspectives on the extraordinary occurrences during this season to share with our children and grandchildren. Thank you for giving us reflections so that others can share and compare. Amen. July 2020.

Journaling COVID-19 Test

Today's opportunity for the coronavirus test takes no pre-arranging. Locations appear every day in the media. There are many free testing sites throughout my community for anyone who decides to accept the test. The areas have increased since the first phases of the pandemic in March 2020. Since I am in the elderly group, I feel compelled to take advantage of this opportunity. I got tested.

If all lives matter, then everyone should be tested for the coronavirus. In any case, experts concur that testing for everybody is not possible. The CDC suggests testing for two primary groups: people showing symptoms (fever, cough, shortness of breath) and those close to an infected person.

COVID-19 can affect anyone, and the disease causes symptoms ranging from mild to very serious from varying risk factors. The CDC is conducting disease examinations and field investigations to understand why some people are more likely to develop severe COVID-19 illness. Risk factors include age, race, gender, medical conditions, medications, poverty, crowding, occupations, and pregnancy. People with certain risk factors might be more likely to need hospitalization and intensive care if they have COVID-19 or more likely to die from the contamination.

In March, I went to the same testing site as today and requested a test. The doctor inquired about my symptoms. I disclosed to her I had none. She then asked my purpose for needing a test. I gave her my age and said we had a two-month-old granddaughter and wanted to see her. The doctor told me I could see the infant and added that the grownups should concern me. Keep your distance from them. Today's open door for the coronavirus test welcomed me with a short line of cars. The test is simple as it's an essential swab taken from your nose. The exam requires a kit, specialized equipment, and trained personnel. Within two to seven days, results appear online. A medical adviser will explain the following steps if the test is positive. I pray my test shows negative.

"Peace I leave with you; my peace I give you. I do not give to you as the world gives. Do not let your hearts be troubled, and do not be afraid" (John 14:27).

Prayer: Heavenly Father, give us the mental fortitude to press forward during this coronavirus pandemic. Scientists say the world is still in a pandemic as the number of cases and deaths increases daily. Help individuals who need to work and open their businesses to stimulate the economy and return to healthy living. Relieve our restless hearts. Help us accept your better ways of living that will bring us peace. Thank you for calming our fears. Amen. July 2020.

Journaling My Test Results

I got tested for COVID-19. It took less than an hour as only three vehicles were ahead. A young medical aid gathered data by looking at our driver's licenses and medical cards. We held them up for him to view as he did not touch them, and there was limited talking. He asks for our email addresses and phone numbers for contact information. In two days, my husband received his results. In four days, I received my results. Both were negative. For positive test results, a medical adviser explains specific steps.

In July, as the coronavirus continues to spread, testing is open for anyone, especially if you have been in the company of a person who tested positive. One day after lunch at a friend's home with three other women, we learned that a common beautician had tested positive for COVID-19. All three of us got negative results. The test reports say "SARS-CoV-2—Not Detected."

Learning of the beautician's positive test appears to fit into one strategy for preventing the spread of COVID-19. Contact tracing identifies individuals with the coronavirus and the people they have been in contact. Should any contacts have the coronavirus, they must see a doctor and, more than likely, self-quarantine at home.

Contact tracers help contain the coronavirus by contacting persons testing positive and determining where they have been and who they were around. The focus is on close contacts or people inside six feet of the infected person for at least ten minutes. Contact tracing begins with identifying everyone a person recently diagnosed with COVID-19 has been in contact with since they became contagious. This strategy reaches out to contain the coronavirus.

"God is our refuge and strength, an ever-present help in trouble. Therefore we will not fear, though the earth gives way and the mountains fall into the heart of the sea" (Ps 46: 1–2).

Prayer: Heavenly Father, the wrath of COVID-19 is completely changing our lives as we know them around the earth. Guide the contact tracers in discovering people who test positive to help stop the spread of the coronavirus. We pray for the medicine to heal those who are infected. We pray for peace for families who are mourning deaths. Please remain our refuge as this pandemic pushes trouble and disarray. Please help us in this crisis to withstand whatever it takes to survive and return to our regular lives. Thank you for giving us the strength to persevere through this pandemic season. Amen. July 2020.

Journaling a Positive COVID-19 Test Result

It was such a pleasure to learn of my negative test results for CO-VID-19 that I did not consider the alternative. What should I have done if the test were positive?

Some doctors and dignitaries get tested daily. Should I get tested again, and the results are positive? What must I do? The CDC says staying home and avoiding other people is critical. Suppose no symptoms evolve. Quarantine for ten days before going around other people. When I tested negative, the information said, "If you test positive, you will be contacted via phone." Then someone will ask for advice from healthcare providers, who will likely request additional testing before considering advanced care. To further complicate things, two sorts of tests are accessible for COVID-19: viral and antibody. Testing negative for COVID-19 by a viral test means there was no infection. However, that does not mean sickness will not occur. An antibody test might indicate a past condition and not a current virus because it can take one to three weeks after infection to make antibodies. Having antibodies to the virus that causes COVID-19 might prevent you from getting infected again. Whether positive or negative for COVID-19 on a viral or an antibody test, I must take preventive measures to protect myself and others. No matter what, I shall stay home, wear a mask in public, wash my hands frequently, and adhere to social distancing.

"Trust in the Lord with all your heart and lean not on your understanding; in all your ways, submit to him, and he will make your paths straight" (Prov 3:5–6).

Prayer: Heavenly Father, COVID-19 test results generate more and more questions about whether the results are positive or negative. We trust you, Lord, as such tests surpass our understanding. We lay all our concerns before you and request your direction while trying to withstand this coronavirus season's trauma. Please send good health to the bodies of all individuals who are affected. We thank you in advance for dismissing COVID-19 from the face of the Earth. Amen. July 2020.

Journaling—COVID-19 Testing Impacts All Our Lives

Testing. Testing! Testing? According to Johns Hopkins University, there are 4.3 million cases of COVID-19 and nearly 155,000 deaths. The consequences of testing guide our economy, joblessness, schools, and federal financial aid.

Six months ago, the CDC analyzed the first coronavirus case in the US. From that point forward, we have been adhering to stay at home, wearing masks in public, washing hands frequently, and social distancing.

Now the mandate is to get tested while we wait for a cure. Testing is now accessible across the country, despite problems that lead to long waits for receiving results. In some communities, it may take two to fourteen days. If you must wait two to fourteen days, you may need another test. The positive test results lowered the stock market, increased unemployment, complicated returning to school, and deliberated federal funding.

The Dow Jones and the FTSE (Financial Times Stock Exchange Group) fell in value as many COVID-19 cases developed. Movements in financial markets can influence the value of pensions or individual savings and small investment accounts. Accordingly, the Federal Reserve Board cut interest rates, making borrowing less expensive and urging spending to improve the economy.

The coming of the coronavirus brought about many people seeking work as they lost their jobs when advised to stay at home and shelter in place. The travel industry, hospitality, restaurants, retail, and entertainment stand still. Today, approximately 10.4% of people in the US are unemployed, as indicated by the International Monetary Fund (IMF). As individuals begin to work in essential industries, there are some signs of recovery.

It remains unclear how students will return to the classroom or college campuses if they are not taking virtual classes in schools. Educational officials are exploring alternative reopening strategies. Some in-person precautions will incorporate regular temperature checks, physical distancing, mask-wearing, alternative schedules, and limitations on gathering places, for example, having lunch. Regardless of the plans, all concur that schools may have to close if the strategy is not working or a new coronavirus outbreak ensues.

Republicans' HEALS Act (Health, Economic Assistance, Liability Protection, and Schools Act) and Democrat's HEROES Act (Health and Economic Recovery Omnibus Emergency Solutions Act) agree on another $1,200 stimulus check for American workers. However, other parts of the Acts differ. American families need financial aid to stave off evictions, utility, and mortgage payments due tomorrow.

"Wait for the Lord; be strong, take heart, and wait for the Lord" (Ps 27:14).

Prayer: Heavenly Father, COVID-19 test results are impacting our economy, employment, and schools, thereby harming the livelihood of families. We pray that government money will come soon to help the people in need. We trust you to be our refuge as we endure this pandemic worldwide. Give us patience as we wait for the end of this coronavirus season. Help us be strong and take heart as we wait for you, Lord. Send a cure that will heal all individuals who are sick. We thank you in advance for ending COVID-19 from the world. Amen. July 2020.

Journaling for COVID-19 Cases and Deaths to Lessen

The numbers and the data show the pandemic is yet with us as testing laboratories punch out test results. But the number of new cases and deaths might be leveling off in some communities. New York is the model state with the most significant lessening numbers.

This information gives me hope. Many government health-related entities provide daily data, which changes weekly. Death certificate data incorporates pneumonia, influenza, and CO-VID-19. The percentage of deaths due specifically to COVID-19 was lower than two weeks but above the pandemic threshold. The number of COVID-19 tests originates from public health laboratories in the United States. The percentage of positive tests indicates as the outbreak progresses, the data interpretation may need to change for new cases. The specific COVID-19 numbers must lessen to visualize any end in sight.

COVID-19 mandates that we hope and pray because of how the virus affects our lives. I will write a daily prayer in my journal and focus on the essential parts of worship: praying for others and myself, asking for forgiveness and thanking God for his blessings.

"Now faith is confidence in what we hope for and assurance about what we do not see" (Heb 11:1).

Prayer: Heavenly Father, the COVID-19 pandemic continues to render havoc upon our economy, employment, and schools, thus destroying the livelihood of families. In faith, we trust you to end this pandemic around the globe. The lessening numbers give us hope as we wait for this coronavirus season. Help us maintain our faith as we see only a glimmer of hope in the data as we wait for you, Lord. Send a cure that will heal all individuals who are sick. We thank you in advance for ending COVID-19 from the world. Amen. August 2020.

COVID-19 Numbers are Lessening

Nationally, surveillance indicators tracking the COVID-19 pandemic levels of associated illnesses, hospitalizations, and deaths remain elevated but show decreasing trends in recent weeks.

We pray these trends reflect a lessening of deaths. We have seen statistics showing far too many are passing away from the pandemic. We have witnessed our loved ones as they lived good lives. We watched them share the wealth. We see the results of the wisdom they communicated. We still feel their love. Thousands have died. We need peace as we grieve in this time of grief. We need blessings for the lives of those the COVID-19 attacked and did not take away.

"You can trust the Lord to protect you. He will not let you fall into harm" (Prov 3:26). "The path of those who live right is like the early morning light. It gets brighter and brighter until the whole light of day" (Prov 4:18).

Prayer: Heavenly Father, we thank you for the opportunity to learn about our friends, family members, and the famous and infamous that live under your protection without harm until you call them home. We thank you for picking them up in the early morning light and taking them to heaven's home. Please ensure those who were hurt or those who died from COVID-19 see the whole light of day in paradise or on earth. Thank you for allowing us to understand that you remain in charge, and the numbers are decreasing. Thank you for helping us stay the course of righteousness and exist in your light. Amen. August 2020.

CHAPTER 2

Observations, Bible Verses, and Prayers

"Hungering for clarity and accord,
I watched COVID-19 counts increase to thousands,
then mourned for those who passed from such discord."

A Million People Have Passed Away

COVID-19 HAS TAKEN MORE than one million lives around the world. Fires in the West continue taking lives and destroying property. The first of three presidential debates begin tonight. We pray for healing, peace, and comfort for all stressed families.

I pray that God hears our cries for a coronavirus cure and calms the fires. I pray for the restoration of our country in all ways. I pray for wisdom and protection from evil.

"For I am the Lord your God who takes hold of your right hand and says to you, do not fear; I will help you" (Isa 41:13).

Prayer: Our Father God, you are our ultimate helper when we are sad, in need, stressed, or overly exuberant. You quell our fears. Stay close to us and hold our hands tightly so they won't slip away from you. We pray for your help dealing with the coronavirus, calming the fires, and guiding our nation's leaders. Please help us. Thank you for helping us get through each day, no matter what. Amen.

The Pandemic Continues

The pandemic continues around the world and takes more lives each day. We pray for a vaccine to end the coronavirus that is causing stress to people with healthcare issues, employment, and school-age children. Storms in the South and fires in the West continue taking lives and destroying property. Election Day is four weeks away. We pray for a fair election.

I pray that God gives ear to the sound of our voices and stands as our refuge in this time of trouble spawned by the coronavirus and raging fires and storms. I pray for patience as we cry for a return to days gone by or new days you send forth.

"But if we hope for what we do not yet have, we wait for it patiently. In the same way, the Spirit helps us in our weaknesses" (Rom 8:25).

Prayer: Our Father God, give us, as your people, patience to withstand all that is happening in the world as we do not understand. We pray that you will help us in our weakness and pray on our behalf, as we do not know what to pray. Intercede in your way. Search our hearts and hear our cries and pleas. You know our needs. Let your will be done, and we will give you praise. Thank you. Amen.

Pray Vaccines Are Forthcoming

COVID-19 cases and deaths increased after a brief period when we thought they were leveling off. We pray for vaccines forthcoming to eliminate the coronavirus stressors on all of us due to unexpected issues we never imagined.

I pray that God will meet our needs as we stand crying for the simple things in our lives. Every day, I pray for patience to wait for a return to days gone by or new days filled with peace and joy.

"So do not throw away this confident trust in the Lord. Remember the great reward it brings you! Patient endurance is what you need now, so that you will continue to do God's will. Then you will receive all he has promised" (Heb 10:35–36).

Prayer: Our Father God, we have confidence in you as believers. We continue to ask for patience to withstand all that is happening. We have no idea what our country will be after the upheaval of the elections, pandemics, storms, fires, protests, and financial disarray. We are trying to endure this worldwide upheaval in hopes that you will reward us with your favor. We believe that you are still in charge. Let your will be done as we are committed to going forward, living by your promises, and knowing peace and joy are forthcoming. Thank you. Amen.

CDC Approves Vaccines

According to the CDC, the FDA has approved two vaccines to prevent COVID-19: Pfizer-BioNTech COVID-19 vaccine and Moderna's COVID-19 vaccine. There should be enough vaccines for all who want vaccinations by summer.

We prayed for God to dismiss the pandemic and send a cure. We thank God for answering our prayer with COVID-19 vaccines. We prayed for guidance for our country's leadership. We thank God for the elected president, vice president, and others addressing our country's needs. We prayed for our lives to return to normal. We thank God for a new normal that is forthcoming.

"People can plan what they want to do, but it is the Lord who guides their steps" (Prov 16:9). "The Lord sees what happens everywhere. He watches everyone, good and evil" (Prov 15:3).

Prayer: Our Father God, thanks for your promise to watch over us. Thanks for getting us through the year-long pandemic and rendering a vaccine. We praise you for eyes of goodness that look upon your chosen ones and others so everyone can feel your presence. We are grateful that you steer our country's paths and correct our wrongs. Continue to discipline our walk with you, so we may not be led astray by unnecessary desires ahead. Please help us walk in wisdom and make the best of our lives. Amen.

We Are Wearying during Uncontrollable Events

For eight months, our country has suffered from losing lives and land due to COVID-19, fires, and storms spreading into new places. We are wearying during these uncontrollable events that render pain and loss. We pray for a return to peace and calm in our environment.

We need patience as your followers are committed to waiting on you. We trust that your will shall be done on earth as it is in heaven. We believe in you.

"But they that wait upon the Lord shall renew their strength; they shall mount up with wings as eagles; they shall run, and not be weary; and they shall walk and not faint" (Isa 40:31).

Prayer: Our Father God, how excellent is thy name. Give ear to the sound of our voices as we call on you to dismiss the relentless nationwide calamities. We believe that if we trust in you wholeheartedly, you will direct our paths and grant us the patience to wait on you. Renew our strength. Increase our abilities to await your direction. Our faith knows the unforeseen is ahead. Our soul waits for you because you are our help and shield. Amen.

Praying for a New Normal

We pray to return to our everyday lives while looking toward a new normal for the country. As more and more people receive doses of the COVID-19 vaccine each day, restaurants and other closed businesses are reopening. More stimulus funds are forthcoming as students return to school buildings and families plan summer vacations.

Things are looking somewhat as expected after a tumultuous year. We are thankful for our blessings.

"He has given us far more than we ask for and more than we deserve. More joy comes each morning" (Prov 20:24). "The night may be filled with tears, but in the morning, we can sing for joy!" (Ps 30:5).

Prayer: Our Father God, thank you for giving us the remedies for COVID-19. We are grateful for receiving far more than we deserve. The gift of more funds to help in our daily lives brings us joy. The pandemic still diverts numerous aspects of our lives while taking other lives. Yet, we gain pure pleasure when things feel wrong and then go right, knowing you will lead us toward joy in the morning. Thank you for caring for us. Amen.

Candidates Run for a Position

This week, President Donald Trump is leading the Republican National Committee Conference to show his work over the last four years and ask people to vote for him. Last week presidential candidate Vice President Joe Biden and vice presidential candidate Senator Kamala Harris presented their case before the world.

One set of candidates will win. They have formidable tasks ahead. With COVID-19 still around, our concerns remain about the economy, schools, voting, jobs, racial justice, and financial help. We pray for a coronavirus cure. We pray for accurate election results in November. We pray for a leadership team to do remarkable things in the coming years.

"So in everything, do to others what you would have them do to you, for this sums up the Law and the Prophets" (Matt 7:12).

Prayer: Our Father God, I cannot assist our nation and its leaders, but I can see they need your direction. Guide them, be with them as they make decisions, and tread new territories in helping our country. Strengthen them and do something they would not believe. Show your Holy Spirit is present. Thank you for blessing our elected leaders. Amen.

Campaigning in Full Force

This week marks the first week of full-time campaigning for the presidency. President Donald Trump and Vice President Mike Pence are seeking to retain their positions. Presidential candidate former Vice President Joe Biden and vice presidential candidate Senator Kamala Harris are endeavoring to unseat Trump and Pence.

Biden and Harris have the challenge to unseat the incumbents with COVID-19 looming. Our concerns remain about the economy, schools, voting, elections, jobs, racial justice, economic issues, and family financial help.

"Now this is what the Lord Almighty says: 'Give careful thought to your ways'" (Hag 1:5).

Prayer: Our Father God, bestow upon the candidates your gifts of wisdom, understanding, counsel, knowledge, and fear of you. Help them use these attributes to present themselves, their platforms, and their promises to the voters. Inspire each one with a sense of integrity and an appreciation for honesty. Please help them to give careful thought to their ways. Thank you in advance for a fair election. Amen.

It's Election Day

Today is Election Day in the United States of America.

Companies are boarding up their stores in areas where protests may lead to riots and looting, regardless of the election outcome. We pray for peace and calm. We trust that God's will shall be done on earth as in heaven. We pray for guidance as we vote for our government leaders.

"The Lord is a refuge for the oppressed, a stronghold in times of trouble. Those who know your name trust in you, for you, Lord, have never forsaken those who seek you" (Ps 9:9–10).

Prayer: Our Father God, we continue to call on you for a fair election today, with no need for lawyers to question the outcome. We pray that you have input into selecting the president and other officials. We ask that you steer all US citizens toward peace and acceptance as we look to you and see your will being done. Bless this nation. Amen.

Electoral College Votes for President

On December 14, 2020, all fifty states and the District of Columbia certified their electoral college votes for president and vice president. Congress will count those electoral votes on January 6, 2021, and president-elect Biden will be inaugurated as the forty-sixth president on January 20 at noon.

I pray for a peaceful transition and a nation of calm and gratitude for our existing democracy. We need the moral benefits of wisdom.

> My son, if you accept my words and store up my commands within you, turning your ear to wisdom and applying your heart to understanding—indeed, if you call out for insight and cry aloud for mercy, and if you look for it as for silver and search for it as for hidden treasure, you will understand the fear of the Lord and find the knowledge of God. For the Lord gives wisdom; from his mouth come knowledge and understanding. He holds success in store for the upright, and he is a shield to those whose walk is blameless, for he guards the course of the just and protects the way of his faithful ones. (Prov 2:1–8)

Prayer: Our Father God, we remain before you, watching the leadership transfer in our nation play out. Even though one more step is fundamental, we cannot yet say it is done. We ask that you award wisdom to our leaders and offer them insight. Keep us near you as we travel this course toward peace and harmony among all men regardless of political or social convictions. Deliver us from the pandemic and any remaining evil lurking among us. Let thy will be done on earth as you determine. Amen.

New Leadership 2021

Our country's government has changed with new leadership in less than seven days. Regardless of a dark day on January 6, when a mob besieged the Capitol, we inaugurated the forty-sixth president, Joe Biden, and his vice president, Kamala Harris. We expect them to accept the mandate of the electorate.

The 117th United States Congress represents the Senate and House of Representatives. The 2020 elections decided that the House of Representatives and the Democratic Party retained their majority.

In the Senate, Republicans hold 50 seats, the Democrats have 48, and two seats by independents that join with the Democrats, effectively making it a 50-50 split. Vice President Kamala Harris serves as the tiebreaker as senate president. The Democrats control the Senate, thereby giving them complete control of Congress.

We pray that blessings surround our leadership to enable them to move onward with new visions and less friction through dialogue and peaceful change.

"But whoever listens to me will live safely and be at ease, without fear of harm" (Prov 1:33).

Prayer: Our Father God, we intend to listen and obey, but the influence of some others leads us astray. Please guide us. Order the leaders' steps so that we may always follow you. Thank you for your promise of security without dread of disaster. Amen.

Justice and Fairness

Across the country, people are speaking up and looking out for others who are not getting justice or fairness. We see individuals trying to prevent the continuation of misguided injustice from all avenues.

The year 2020 made us tired and weary. Many are doing necessary work as government leaders, scientists, physicians, economists, and communicators look out for all. Even though there is much more to do, those who seek God and follow him never complain that we have lost our way. Instead, we look out for one another because we believe God will protect us when we follow him.

"Come to me all of you who are tired from the heavy burden you have been forced to carry. I will give you rest. Accept my teaching. Learn from me. I am gentle and humble in spirit. And you will be able to get some rest. Yes, the teaching that I ask you to accept is easy. The load I give you to carry is light" (Matt 11:28–30). "He gives good advice to honest people and shields those who do what is right He makes sure that people are treated fairly. He watches over His loyal followers" (Prov 2:7–8).

Prayer: Our Father God, thank you for your promise to ensure your people treat one another fairly. We are your faithful followers. Protect those around us and let them feel your presence through us. Please, give us your guidance to do what is right. Amen.

He's Making It Right

It's unnecessary to list the myriad subjects we covered in our crises to the Lord. Remember the goodness he bestowed upon us. He rendered blessings. Despite the COVID-19 pandemic and its impact on our health, economy, and government, we trusted our Father. We didn't understand then; now we see he's making life more livable.

There were many significant occurrences in 2020: Black Lives Matter got people talking about racism following the death of George Floyd; afterward, a jury found the policeman guilty. The voters elected Joe Biden as president and Kamala Harris as vice president. The #MeToo movement brought many prominent men to see their inappropriate actions before the public. The administration provided stimulus funds to its citizens. God is continuing to make it right.

"The righteous person is rescued from trouble, and it falls on the wicked instead" (Prov 11:8).

Prayer: Our Father God, we have prayed for our country and the world during the COVID-19 pandemic. With our heads bowed, eyes closed, and bodies bent, we submitted pleas for all things impacting our lives. Thanks for vaccines to fight the coronavirus and for correcting things that impacted our lives during the pandemic. We try to follow your guidance and act according to the gift of knowledge you have given us. Please help us be right-minded as we adjust to the new boundaries you provide. Thank you for our new everyday lives. Amen.

A Time for Everything

We call upon our heavenly Father asking for healing grace to restore our physical and mental health and broken hearts as we grieve for our lost loved ones. He knows where we need healing to cover every broken place and relieve our pain and suffering.

"There is a time for everything, and a season for every activity under the heavens: a time to be born and a time to die, a time to plant and a time to uproot, a time to kill and a time to heal" (Eccl 3:1–3).

Prayer: Our Father God, render your healing upon us. Give us the patience to wait until you decide the time. You make everything beautiful in its time. We thank you for being willing to do more than we could ever imagine. Forgive us for not acknowledging how much we need you above everything. We love you for showing us your excellent glory in your time. Amen.

Become Stronger

As we adjust to this coronavirus season, let us look forward to becoming stronger individuals.

"And the God of all grace, who called you to his eternal glory in Christ, after you have suffered a little while, will himself restore you and make you strong, firm, and steadfast" (1 Pet 5:10).

Prayer: Our Father God, forgive us for grumbling during our suffering in this pandemic season. We give our past to you, so you can guide us to walk in your ways in the future. Make us learn from our experiences and become more assertive in our endeavors for you. Thank you for your steadfast strength. Amen.

We Witness Miracles Daily

The Bible reports many miracles done by faith. All of those wonders led to something extraordinary. We remember a few: walking on water, feeding the five thousand, raising Lazarus from the dead, changing water into wine, catching a large number of fish, calming a stormy sea, and the resurrection.

When thinking about faith, we refer to the definition as "the confidence in what we hope for and assurance about what we do not see" (Heb 11.1).

Today, we don't see faith in the same way. We have so much automation and various resources we miss the opportunity to witness the miracles. Yet, many events may be in the phenomenon or wonder class in the past year.

The coronavirus spread worldwide, spinning economies out of control, yet we survived that pandemic. The United States and other countries are protesting fair and free elections, but democracy prevails. Climate disruptions continue as we envision the intensity of a new climate typical. Stimulus funds are distributed to people to avoid hunger and strife. Injustice is being addressed for racial inequities as the world looks on.

Now we need faith. With so many miraculous happenings, we don't even realize our faith, which is a gift from God. "For it is by grace you have been saved, through faith—and this is not from yourselves, it is the gift of God—not by works, so that no one can boast" (Eph 2:8–9). "For in the gospel, the righteousness of God is revealed—a righteousness that is by faith from first to last, just as it is written: The righteous will live by faith" (Rom 1:17).

Prayer: Our Father God, help us live by the faith you supply. Direct us to pray for the people yet mourning the dead from COVID-19 issues and others you called home. Bless those in poor mental states from a year of pandemic stillness. Grant wisdom to those in leadership positions. Give us confidence that you will continue to bestow the desires of our hearts upon us. Thank you for being so gracious. Amen.

We Are Thankful for Blessings

We pray to return to our everyday lives while looking to a new normal for the country. As more and more people receive doses of the COVID-19 vaccine each day, restaurants and other closed businesses are reopening.

Additional stimulus funds will help businesses reopen and allow new businesses to start. We have so much for which to be thankful. As we see more and more people out and about and children playing on playgrounds, there appears to be a sense of gratitude in the air.

"The Lord guides our steps, and we never know where he will lead us" (Prov 20:24). "If we delight ourselves in the Lord and commit our ways to the Lord, He will give us the desires of our hearts" (Ps 37:4).

Prayer: Our Father God, thank you for your promise to guide our steps. The pandemic still diverts numerous aspects of our lives while taking other lives. We are neither wearing masks as we should nor standing a safe distance from others. Yet, we feel your presence, knowing that you are leading our way. We thank you for giving us the direction necessary to follow your correct path. Thank you for you guiding our steps. Amen.

Prayer Changes Things

COVID-19 continues to rage around the world. Fires in the West are taking lives and destroying property. Political campaigns are separating people into definitive groups. Yet I believe prayer changes things

I pray that God hears our cries for a coronavirus cure and calms the fires. I pray for the restoration of our country into our new lives. I pray for wisdom, protection, and understanding.

"Be very careful, then, how you live—not as unwise but as wise, making the most of every opportunity, because the days are evil. Therefore do not be foolish, but understand what the Lord's will is" (Eph 5:15–17).

Prayer: Our Father God, we have let many opportunities pass because we were not focused on you. Help us be careful as we search for more opportunities amid the pandemic. We pray for restoration from this coronavirus and wisdom for our nation's leaders. Please render us an understanding of your will. Thank you for helping us through each day filled with natural fires and ongoing protests that kill and destroy. Amen.

CHAPTER 3

Spiritually Speaking
Acknowledgments and Prayers

"I called for Mercy to save those in houses.
Examining my impatience each day
with more burdens in education
and in elder care and prisons to stay."

Vaccines for Prevention

THE THIRD LETTER OF John 1:2 says, "Beloved, I pray that all may go well with you and that you may be in good health, just as it is well with your soul."

Many who have not taken a vaccine for COVID-19 cite their religion, historical events, and sheer reticence. I have received both initial Pfizer vaccines and the booster, and I continue to wear my mask. I am encouraging you to do the same. I want all of us to remain in good health.

According to Kaiser Family Foundation's surveys, four percent of Americans intend to get vaccinated as soon as possible but haven't yet. Another twelve percent are in wait-and-see mode. Many of them are the same people who are anti-vaccine and consider mask mandates violations of their civil rights.

Some Black Americans express little trust in the healthcare system as they remember abuses, like the Tuskegee study in which Black people were experimented on without their consent.

Currently, they continue to encounter discrimination from doctors and hospitals.

If enough people don't get vaccinated, the threat of COVID-19 and its variants could continue for years. Then, what can we say to our children, who need to be vaccinated and wear masks in school? What can we say to our parents and grandparents who may be at risk due to age and physical impairment? We cannot hurt those we love by not getting vaccinated.

Almost eighty percent of adults in the United States have received at least one dose of the virus vaccine, and COVID-19 cases are declining among vaccinated folk. Yet Delta variant cases and hospitalizations are rising among unvaccinated people.

The CDC has indicated that vaccine equity is an important goal. They defined it as preferential access and administration to those most affected by COVID-19. The percentage disparity between white, brown, and Black adults is decreasing.

Some corporations require vaccinations or frequent testing; rapid tests are available in every community. Knowing whether or not you have COVID-19 may help you keep your job or get another one.

We prayed for God to dismiss the pandemic and send help. We thank him for answering our prayers with three COVID-19 vaccines for prevention.

We prayed for our lives to return to normal. We thank God for the new normal that is upon us.

While the Bible seldom mentions doctors, Matt 9:12 says: "Those who are well do not need a physician, but those who are sick." Bible prophets delivered godly messages, helped uncover the reasons for crises, and introduced rituals to bring healing and ensure survival.

In biblical times, it was often more important to address the cause of the disease through a ritual than to find a medical cure. One may not have been able to control their fate, but practices offered some sense of peace and comfort amid catastrophes. We can liken getting vaccinated to a ritual to overcome COVID-19.

"People can plan what they want to do, but it is the Lord who guides their steps" (Prov 16:9). The Lord sees what happens everywhere. He watches everyone—good and evil" (Prov 15:3).

Prayer: Dear Lord, thank you for the promise to watch over us. Thank you for getting us through the pandemic of the last two years and rendering a vaccine. We praise your eyes of goodness that look upon your chosen ones and others so that everyone can feel your presence. We thank you for directing our country's path and correcting our wrongs. Continue to discipline our walk with you so we may not be led astray by ungodly ways. Please help us walk in wisdom and make the best possible use of our lives. Amen.

The Pre-Easter Lenten Season

As observed in many churches, Lent is the forty days Christians prepare to celebrate Jesus' resurrection. Easter ends the Lenten season.

Lent is a period of penitence and fasting. Believers repent of their sins and pledge a commitment to change. According to a *Lifeway* poll, about a quarter of Americans observe Lent (including 61 percent of Catholics and 20 percent of Protestants).[1]

Lent commemorates the forty days Jesus was fasting in the wilderness without water or food on the Christian liturgical calendar. At the same time, Satan tempted him, as described in the Gospels of Matthew, Mark, and Luke.

Fasting, especially when accompanied by prayer and confession, is a way of denying ourselves the excesses and distractions of life so that we might become more aware of the Lord's voice.

The Bible tells of others fasting when petitioning God for something important. For instance, the Israelites "mourned and wept and fasted till evening for Saul and his son Jonathan, and for the army of the Lord and for the nation of Israel, because they had fallen by the sword" (2 Sam 1:12). Before going to her husband to

1. 1. "American Views on Lent" (LifeWay Research, http://research.lifeway.com/wp-content/uploads/2017/02/Sept-2016-American-Views-Lent.pdf).

intercede for the Jews, Esther told Mordecai, "Go, gather together all the Jews who are in Susa, and fast for me. Do not eat or drink for three days, night or day. I and my attendants will fast as you do" (Esth 4:16). Historically, Christians and Jews have fasted to repent, overcome challenges, and seek God's favor.

Now, what do Christians do during the Lenten season? On Ash Wednesday, ministers place ashes on peoples' foreheads to show that those individuals belong to Jesus Christ and are grieving and mourning their sins. We submit special prayers for God to answer and often promise to give up a particular bad habit or excessive activity. On all the Fridays of Lent, we don't eat meat—instead, we eat fish, having countless fish fry dinners at churches.

How am I going to make this Lenten season memorable for me? By fasting and praying. Upon awakening each day, I shall start a prayer with "Dear Lord, I am grateful for . . ." and include "I am prayerful for . . ." On Fridays, I am committed to fasting from meat and from adding sugar to any drinks on all the other days.

As prayer accompanies fasting, I ask God to improve the situations impacting lives worldwide as we prepare for this coming Easter Sunday. Phil 4:6 says, "Do not be anxious about anything, but in everything by prayer and supplication with thanksgiving let your requests be made known to God."

Prayer: Dear God, in this season of Lent, we thank and praise you for easing the pain caused by the pandemic. Now we're anxious as we observe people's daily difficulties and struggles in Ukraine. The way seems too dark and marked by immense grief and pain. We can't see how the Ukrainian people can recover from these circumstances. But amid their weakness, we ask that you be strong on their behalf. Lord, rise. Let your Spirit shine from every broken place. We choose to give you thanks today, believing this season of darkness will fade away. We praise you and think you will make all things new. May your light shine so we can see the good surrounding us and watch Your Holy Spirit create a world of peace? Stretch forth your mighty right hand and be our sure defense. Show us your glory, Lord, now and forever. Amen.

Lent Ends and Holy Week Begins

Palm Sunday is the final Sunday of Lent and the beginning of Holy Week, which commemorates Christ's arrival before the crucifixion. Palms on Sunday recall how people greeted Jesus, carrying palm branches as he entered Jerusalem. "They took branches of palm trees and went out to meet him, shouting, 'Hosanna! Blessed is he who comes in the name of the Lord'" (John 12:13).

What shall we do during the unique pandemic period of Holy Week? Many churches host Holy Communion services on Monday, Tuesday, and Wednesday. People share bread and wine, known as the Eucharist, to remember how Jesus sacrificed his life to atone for human sins. Moreover, reenactments of the events commemorating Jesus' life, especially those leading up to his death, help people recall his last days. At the same time, special services symbolize the discipleship actions of offering prayer for the sick and providing food for those in need.

For Maundy Thursday, Jesus hosted the Last Supper and celebrated the final meal with his disciples. He washed their feet to serve others with humility to encourage them to follow his example. In other words, "copy my humility and love one another as I have loved you." Many churches hold special services that include a meal and washing feet.

During the Last Supper, Jesus gave the disciples his last command, one by which we can all live: "So now I am giving you a new commandment: Love each other. Just as I have loved you, you should love one another. Your love for one another will prove to the world that you are my disciples" (John 13:34–35).

Good Friday commemorates the suffering and death of Jesus Christ on the cross. Many Christians spend Good Friday fasting, praying, repenting, and meditating.

We observe Holy Saturday as the day when Jesus lay in the tomb. As a day of sadness, some hold an Easter vigil service, a forty-hour watch between Good Friday and Easter Sunday.

Easter Sunday, also known as Resurrection Day, is the culmination of Jesus' mission on earth and is summarized in Matt

20:17–19: "Now Jesus was going up to Jerusalem. On the way, he took the Twelve aside and said to them, 'We are going up to Jerusalem, and the Son of Man will be delivered to the chief priests and the law teachers. They will condemn him to death and will hand him over to the Gentiles to be mocked and flogged and crucified. On the third day, he will be raised to life!'"

The Holy Week days between Palm Sunday and Easter give us time to focus our prayers on an end to the pandemic, while remembering Jesus Christ. We pray and remember him as we celebrate the end of the Lenten season and the Resurrection Day, for he promised to go and prepare a place for us. "And if I go and prepare a place for you, I will come back and take you to be with me that you also may be where I am" (John 14:3). Oh Lord, we eagerly await your return. Amen.

Prayer for Mothers

Heavenly Father, we understand we arrived here with your assistance and the direction you gave our mothers. We thank you for bringing us safely to this point in our lives. This outing called life has been challenging, especially with the pandemic, international wars, and many crises you are helping mothers and families navigate.

We recognize the lifeblood you assign to mothers. We cheer in realizing you are the source of our needs and blessings. Thanks for the grace you provide our mothers without them asking. We see you as a living, loving, and forgiving God. We ask that you pardon our wrongdoings, the intentional ones and those we committed by not focusing on the direction you sent through our mothers.

"Only be careful and watch yourselves closely so that you do not forget the things your eyes have seen or let them fade from your heart as long as you live. Teach them to your children and to their children after them" (Deut 4:9).

Please give mothers guidance in childrearing to proceed with diligence and love. Help each one find the eternal significance you place on parenthood. Help her comprehend that a most critical world-changing event may occur through her child, with your direction and care.

Thank you for every mother you have depended on with your valuable children. We appreciate the penance each mother gives for her youngsters with the time she allows, regardless of whether she is a homemaker, working mother, or one who has blended the two.

We particularly appeal to single mothers who must lean exclusively on you for fathering their youngsters. We thank you for encircling children who may never know their natural fathers.

We likewise appeal to those who never had the pleasure of bearing youngsters yet reach out to needy children who enter their lives. "But if you seek the Lord your God from there, you will find him if you seek him with all your heart and soul" (Deut 4:29).

Please touch the hearts of your chosen mothers. Instruct them to be coaches and role models to their children. Guide them. Show mothers how to respond with eagerness, persistence, commitment, and genuine love. Grant them insight and wisdom as we try to endure the pandemic attack.

Prayer: Lord, we ask you to hurl refreshing downpours of favor upon all mothers. Lift their spirits when there is, by all accounts, no explanation in troublesome times. We pray that children observe a difference in their mothers because of your presence within them. We trust that mothers appreciate the opportunity to indulge in motherhood to watch their offspring develop with your help. Dear God, keep our families safe from COVID-19. Amen.

Pentecost

Before Jesus ascended into heaven, He told His followers to stay in Jerusalem and wait for the Holy Spirit. "When the day of Pentecost came, they were all together in one place. Suddenly a sound like the blowing of a violent wind came from heaven and filled the whole house where they were sitting. They saw what seemed to be tongues of fire that separated and came to rest on each of them.

They were filled with the Holy Spirit and began to speak in other tongues as the Spirit enabled them" (Acts 2:1–4).

The Holy Spirit entered Jerusalem to establish his presence to the followers and instructed them to spread the news that Jesus forgives transgressions and reunites sinners to God. Before Pentecost, His disciples hid from the public for fear of persecution. After Pentecost, Jesus' followers felt encouraged to carry on his ministry. Jesus' followers were in Jerusalem when the Holy Spirit arrived. For Christians, Pentecost marks the birthday of the Christian church, the day Peter preached, and in response to that sermon, there was a harvest of many souls converted. Pentecost marks the outpouring of the Holy Spirit that equips us to do the work of God, even now as the pandemic slows its spread.

After 2020, we are rejoicing and thanking God for his many blessings. Shavuot is a Jewish holiday commemorating the giving of the Torah to Moses at Mount Sinai. Since Shavuot occurs fifty days after the first day of Passover, it is sometimes known as Pentecost, a Greek word that means "fifty." The earlier celebrations of Shavuot related to the harvesting season fifty days later. They rejoiced by giving their first fruits to the Temple and thanked God for their material blessings.

"And I will ask the Father, and he will give you another advocate to help and be with you forever— the Spirit of truth. The world cannot accept him because it neither sees nor knows him. But you know him, for he lives with you and will be in you. I will not leave you as orphans; I will come to you" (John 14:16–18).

Prayer: Heavenly Father, thank you for the Spirit of Truth intertwined in our lives. We are inspired to obey you and love you first. We understand your teachings and the indwelling of the Holy Spirit mesh together as one. We are encouraged by the multitude of blessings you bestow upon us, especially the diminishing of the pandemic. We thank God with our hearts and will remind everyone of His wonders. Amid this pandemic, bless our land and all the peoples who dwell upon it. Amen.

Father's Day—We Need Father Figures

We need father figures to give children unconditional love, provide extreme patience, show self-sacrifice, and express encouragement. Fathers in the Bible played notable roles in exemplifying the importance of fatherhood through honesty, strength, and responsibility.

The Bible mentions some exemplary fathers: God the Father; Adam, the first man; Noah, a noble man; Abraham, father of the Jewish people; Jacob, father of the tribes of Israel; King David, who fathered the royal line from which Jesus was born; Joseph, human father of Jesus.

"Fathers, do not aggravate your children, or they will become discouraged" (Col 3:21). "My child, accept the Lord's discipline and don't be upset when he corrects you. For the Lord corrects those he loves, just as a father corrects a child in whom he delights" (Prov 3:11–12).

Prayer: Heavenly Father, we are grateful for the fathers you bestowed upon us. Touch their hearts so they can feel your presence in their lives. Remind them of their children and the need to be present in their lives. Teach them to fulfill the roles you have for them in their children's lives, as we endure this pandemic season. Let them see how to become involved, influential, committed, loving, and model fathers. Heal the hurt that exists between father and offspring. Please show them your glory. Thank you for guiding us to speak kindly about our fathers. Amen.

Frederick Douglass' Fourth of July

The Fourth of July is the celebration of the United States of America's independence. Thomas Jefferson of Virginia led the committee named to draft a proclamation justifying the break with Great Britain. In 1776, the Continental Congress adopted the statement as the Declaration of Independence.

Many people pause to read parts of Frederick Douglass July 5, 1852 speech at national celebrations. Douglass initially delivered the speech at an event commemorating the signing of the Declaration of Independence, held in Rochester, New York.

"What to the Slave is the Fourth of July?" Douglass asked. "This Fourth of July is yours, not mine. . . But, both for your sakes and ours, would to God that an affirmative answer could be truthfully returned to these questions! Then would my task be light and my burden easy and delightful . . . For who is there so cold that a nation's sympathy could not warm him? Who so stolid and selfish would not give his voice to swell the hallelujahs of a nation's jubilee, when the chains of servitude had been torn from his limbs? I am not that man.

But such is not the state of the case. I say it with a sad sense of the disparity between us. I am not included within the pale of glorious anniversary! Your high independence only reveals the immeasurable distance between us. The blessings in which you, this day, rejoice, are not enjoyed in common. The rich inheritance of justice, liberty, prosperity, and independence, bequeathed by your fathers, is shared by you, not by me. The sunlight that brought light and healing to you has brought stripes and death to me. This Fourth of July is yours, not mine. You may rejoice. I must mourn. . ."

On August 28, 1963, Dr. Martin Luther King gave his famous "I Have a Dream" speech on the Mall in Washington, DC. In it, he uttered a memorable line: "Free at last, free at last. Thank God Almighty, we're free at last." These words remain symbolic, yet, fifty eight years later, not much has changed in the tenor of Black lives.

Vandals removed the statue of Frederick Douglass from its base in a park in Rochester, NY, and then dumped it near a river gorge on Sunday, July 5, 2020—the day that marked the 168th anniversary of Douglass Fourth of July speech. Local leaders speculate that the damage might be in reaction to the national concern over minorities damaging Confederate monuments around the country, during the pandemic.

Douglass believed the church could make a difference if we followed the Word. We are supposedly independent people in earthly terms, but we are free because of Jesus and now become dependent upon God in heavenly terms. Douglass told a slave that celebrating Independence Day "reveals to him, more than all other days in the year, the gross injustice and cruelty to which he is the constant victim."

"It is for freedom that Christ has set us free. Stand firm, then, and do not let yourselves be burdened again by a yoke of slavery" (Gal 5:1).

Prayer: Heavenly Father, this federal holiday brings to mind that although slavery ended more than 150 years ago, injustices remain in myriad forms to attack employment, race relations, health care, poverty, gun use, abuse, civil rights, voting rights, and cultural disparities. We persevere daily to take matters into our own hands and correct the wrongs. Because we are unsuccessful, we call upon you for grace and justice and peace for those who encounter injustices. Help us meet your requirements to achieve justice, love, and kindness. Guide us to stand firm with you. Please destroy the pandemic and show us your mercy! Amen.

Is This Your Season?

Is this your season? Get ready for the future, understanding that nothing is new and there is a time for everything.

"Over the past year, we've lived through some of our darkest days. Now, I truly believe . . . I truly believe we're about to see our brightest future. Folks, this is a special nation." President Joe Biden included this statement in his July 4, 2021 speech.[2]

Biden's expression captures our present-day message that the best is yet to come.

The challenges facing our communities are becoming increasingly severe, and it often feels like we will be unable to get through these times. The Great Depression of the 1930s and

---

2. "Remarks by President Biden Celebrating Independence Day and Independence from COVID-19" (Whitehouse.gov, Jul 4, 2021, https://www. whitehouse.gov/briefing-room/speeches-remarks/2021/07/05/remarks-by-president-biden-celebrating-independence-day-and-independence-from-covid-19), para. 36.

the world wars left monumental scars on people, yet we made it through those events.

The most urgent problems are ending the COVID-19 health crisis, health care, getting the economy back on track, workforce development, defense and national security, racial equity, criminal justice, law enforcement, and corporate responsibility. However, even broader challenges are yet to be overcome, such as making our local and national governments work for their citizens, unifying a deeply divided nation, and restoring legitimacy to American democracy in voting.

As we look at our surroundings, we must remind ourselves there is a time for everything. "There is a time for everything and a season for every activity under the heavens" (Eccl 3:1). What do workers gain from their toil? I have seen the burden God has laid on the human race. He has made everything beautiful in its time. He has also set eternity on the human heart. Yet, no one can fathom what God has done from beginning to end" (Eccl 3:9–11).

"Whatever has already been, whatever will be has been before, and God will call the past to account" (Eccl 3:13).

Prayer: Heavenly Father, in your word, it says there is a time for everything when seasons allow all things to happen. There is a time to be born and a time to die as we journey through our lives. If this is how it must be, help us put the past behind us. Knowing that everything happened once in the past gives us some understanding to accept it now and the patience to get through the pandemic dark days. These days we need to address health care, economic assistance, criminal justice and injustice, racial equity, impending wars, and more. Our nation is deeply divided. Unify our people to the point of overall acceptance. We believe you are the great "I Am." We trust you. We believe in the gifts you gave us to eat and drink, and we find satisfaction in our toil. We believe that everything from you will endure forever. Please help us to get through these pandemic seasons. We believe there is a time for everything. Amen.

Newness in September

September is best known for returning to school; it marks a new beginning for students from preschool to postgraduate school. It's a new beginning for new issues when we return to work after our summer vacations. When senior staff and board members finalize the following year's budget and plans, spiritually speaking, given the impact that COVID-19 has had and continues to have on our lives, we must believe that God has another plan for this new fall season. We prepare for it with a fresh outlook clad in refreshed abilities and sharpened tools to do our work.

September requires us to reengage after our summer hiatus. We transform by renewing our minds so that we can meet the test of God's good and perfect will. We have talents to use in our roles as leaders and followers. Jesus was the leader of his disciples, and his disciples were leaders and followers in various positions on their respective journeys. God has given us different gifts like the disciples according to his redeeming grace:

> The Spirit gives one person the ability to speak with wisdom. And the same Spirit gives another person the ability to communicate with knowledge. The Spirit gives faith to one person, giving the gift of healing to another. He offers one person the power to do miracles, another ability to prophesy, and another to judge what is from the Spirit and what is not. The Spirit gives one person the ability to speak in different languages, and to another, he provides the ability to interpret those languages." (1 Cor 12:8–10)

We exercise our God-given gifts daily. Yet, if we are to be strong in the Lord and access his mighty power, we put on his whole armor when we take a stand. We may struggle against authorities, dark forces, negative thinking, and enemies who can do nothing of themselves. In the midst of the pandemic, we recall the following declaration made by the Lord: "For I know the plans I have for you, plans to prosper you and not to harm you, plans to give you hope" (Jer 29:11).

Look around. Can't you see he is doing new things by creating new paths? In the same way, we can do all things through Christ, who has helped us survive the pandemic.

As we engage in its newness, thought and discernment are required. "So whenever you eat, drink, or do anything else, do it all for the glory of God" (1 Cor 10:31).

Prayer: Dear God, we see you as our refuge and ever-present help in times of trouble. Therefore, though the storms flood, fires sweep the land, and the Delta variant has increased the number of infections and is spreading faster than the original COVID-19 strain, we will not fear. We ask you to stand beside us as we move through new paths using the talents you have distributed to each of us. With the newness of this fall season, we're on a journey of learning with many curves. We need your help with our mere being. Guide us as we put our faith in you. Show us the way to joy in the newness of this September. Amen.

Thanksgiving

Those who celebrate Thanksgiving typically go to a designated family member's house to dine until everyone is full. Part of the typical dining ritual requires each person to say thanks aloud for the blessings they experienced during the year.

In 2020, as the pandemic continued, we gathered for Thanksgiving, specifically with those in our homes, with no visits to grandparents in nursing homes. Twenty twenty-one brought vaccinations and provided enough comfort to return to normalcy, including Thanksgiving dinner with guests.

This holiday means different things to different people. In addition to dining on turkey, gravy, and cranberry sauce, some employees take a four-day vacation from Thursday through Sunday. Shoppers stake out stores on Black Friday, one of the year's biggest shopping days. In addition, there are always football and soccer games playing live on television.

Praising God on Thanksgiving Day comes from traditions that began in 1621. After a terrible year in which many people died of starvation and disease, the Pilgrims set aside three days in December to praise the Lord for a bountiful harvest of corn. In 1789, in response to God granting America independence from Britain, President George Washington proclaimed November 26 as a National Day of Thanksgiving unto the Lord. In 1863, Abraham Lincoln called more attention to this tradition of giving thanks. Finally, in 1941, the United States Congress decreed the fourth Thursday of November as a national holiday.

Thanksgiving is one of my favorite times, and Ps 107 is my reminder. Verse 1 says, "Give thanks to the Lord, for he is good, his love endures forever." Verses 21–22 say, "Let them give thanks to the Lord for his unfailing love and his wonderful deeds for men. Let them sacrifice thank offerings and tell of his works with songs of joy."

We have so much for which to be thankful. In spite of the pandemic, we welcome a fresh new day that every morning brings, a newborn baby's cry, the love we feel when we encounter a beloved one, and the joy we feel when the Lord forgives our sins and answers our prayers. We should "rejoice always, pray continually, give thanks in all circumstances; for this is God's will for you in Christ Jesus" (1 Thess 5:16–18).

Prayer: Dear Heavenly Father, we are grateful as we shout joyfully for the subsiding of the pandemic, and we are discovering new ways of living, working, and caring for one another. Looking back, we can see that you have done glorious things throughout the earth. We ask that you continue to help us avoid being anxious about anything. Still, with prayer and gratitude, we appreciate the opportunity to share with others on Thanksgiving our remembrances filled with love and laughter that have taken us through the past two years. We praise you for giving us the gift of patience to get through the pandemic's life-changing events. We thank you for your indescribable gift of goodness and abounding love, which endures forever. Amen.

Christmas

From Thanksgiving until Christmas, we celebrate an extraordinary season. The pandemic has brought families closer together. It feels like a conspiracy of love. "For God so loved the world, that he gave his only Son, that whoever believes in him should not perish but have eternal life" (John 3:16).

It's Christmastime. The word Christmas comes from Cristes maesse, Old English for "Christ's Mass," which refers to the Catholic tradition of holding a special mass ceremony to celebrate Jesus.

We intentionally engage with one another during these forty days and define goodwill by saying kind words, lending helping hands, and giving gifts. Amid all the giving, we sometimes remember that Christmas celebrates Christ's birth on December 25th. Gifting acknowledges God's sending us the gift of his Son. Also, three wise men visited the newborn Jesus and brought gifts for him. A poem titled "A Visit from St. Nicholas," penned in 1822, popularized the tradition of exchanging gifts as we do today.

Nine out of ten people in America celebrate Christmas as the holiday season for gathering and sharing.[3] By name, it is a holiday for Christians. Most Christmas traditions vary in religious and symbolic meaning. Non-believing agnostics, atheists, and non-Christians connect by giving and receiving gifts because it is a family time with and without biblical implications. Even with COVID-19, we celebrate Christmas while remembering to express our gratitude for this time with friends and family and hope, peace, love, and joy.

The book of Matthew conveys the account of a young girl giving birth to Jesus Christ, the Son of God.

> Now the birth of Jesus Christ was as follows: after his mother Mary was betrothed to Joseph, before they came together, she was found with child of the Holy Spirit. Then Joseph her husband, being a just man, and not

3. Lipka, Michael, and David Masci, "5 Facts about Christmas in America" (Pew Research, Dec 18, 2017, https://www.pewresearch.org/fact-tank/2017/12/18/5-facts-about-Christmas-in-america), para. 3.

wanting to make her a public example, was minded to put her away secretly. But while he thought about these things, behold, an angel of the Lord appeared to him in a dream, saying, "Joseph, Son of David, do not be afraid to take to you Mary your wife, for that which is conceived in her is of the Holy Spirit. And she will bring forth a Son, and you shall call His name Jesus, for He will save His people from their sins."

So all this was done that it might be fulfilled which was spoken by the Lord through the prophet, saying: "Behold, the virgin shall be with child, and bear a Son, and they shall call His name Immanuel," which is translated, "God with us."

Then Joseph, being aroused from sleep, did as the angel of the Lord commanded him and took to him his wife, and did not know her till she had brought forth her first-born Son. And he called His name Jesus. (Matt 1:18–25)

Prayer: Heavenly Father, thank you for giving us your Son in human form. We are taking time now during this Christmas season to celebrate his birth. As we rejoice with one another, we remember to applaud Jesus as the reason for these special days. Grant peace in our homes and hearts during this new pandemic season. Thank you for the chance to celebrate the same gifts of hope, peace, love, and joy you sent to us during the advent of his first coming. We give you praise, glory to God in the highest, peace, and goodwill toward men on earth. Amen.

New Year's Resolution

Making a New Year's resolution is an annual exercise whereby we promise to do something different to enhance our lives in the new year. Regardless of our good intentions for the coming year, we can easily overlook our most significant need: to improve our prayer life by reaching out to God. We need his grace and power to carry out his will for each of us with or without the pandemic.

Common New Year's resolutions include losing weight, exercising, quitting smoking, getting more rest, drinking more water, drinking less alcohol, or paying off—or simply no longer using—credit cards. While your resolution might be one of these, I resolve to be grateful and prayerful this year.

I plan to host a daily personal adoration session during which I tell God I am grateful and pray about something. My expression of gratefulness is saying thanks. My prayerfulness is an earnest hope or a wish for help in some endeavor. My goal is to put a spiritual intercession into practice, which is critical to my Christian life.

Simply put, I want to improve my relationship with God through communication. Prayer represents the way we communicate with him. It is more than making a special request and waiting for his answer. God calls us to pray to maintain a relationship with him. In 1 Thess 5:17, he says to "pray continually."

God also reminds us of his commitment to developing and deepening our relationship with him in Isa 41:10: "So do not fear, for I am with you; do not be dismayed, for I am your God. I will strengthen and help you; I will uphold you with my righteous right hand."

If I want to maintain this New Year's commitment for the entire year, I must speak to God in prayer every day. When I open my eyes in the morning, a simple "good morning, Lord" is a respectful start. Since my focus is on being grateful and prayerful, I must also thank him for something special or the joy of waking to see another day that he has made. As I choose to be prayerful, I make a request or ask, "Lord, what would you have me do for you today?"

The rest of my day will take care of itself as I continue to pray while staying in touch with God in all my actions and conversations with others. "Even if I walk through a valley as dark as the grave, I will not be afraid of any danger because you are with me. Your rod and staff comfort me" (Ps 23:4).

I have faith in his message no matter how the pandemic is happening to me. "I have good plans for you. I don't plan to hurt you. I plan to give you hope and a promising future" (Jer 29:11).

Prayer: With the words of his promise to me, I pray that I will conduct myself so that someone will recognize his face in mine every day. I pray that my faith in him will not falter, and I live as if I trust his word. I pray that I will enjoy the grace, peace, and comfort he gives me each day during the pandemic. Amen.

He's Giving Us a New Year

As we move into 2022, God is yet speaking to us. He's giving us a new year, guaranteed to be filled with his presence. Listen for him.

After two difficult years, we are all truly blessed to feel some ease in moving about, perhaps some peace and comfort in our surroundings. The pandemic has altered our lives forever, and we thank God for a brand-new year that will undoubtedly include positive and negative events ahead that we cannot fathom. With new COVID strains, we're praying for the best and preparing for the worst by getting vaccinated and boosted.

Omicron COVID appears to be a less symptomatic variant but is still contagious. More people were getting tests and quarantined faster with fewer hospitalizations and deaths. Many companies, organizations, and schools require vaccinations to reduce the spread.

COVID has changed the world, but God has not changed. He promised that his goodness was a consistent reality in life. "'I am the Alpha and the Omega,' says the Lord God, 'who is, and who was, and who is to come, the Almighty'" (Rev 1:8).

During the past two years, God has spoken to us, and we listen as he continues to talk to us in 2022. "For when he spoke, the world began! It appeared at his command" (Ps 33:9). Through the pandemic, our world started anew. These recent times have turned us upside down and around in different ways. We've learned that some things are not essential, and we remember to listen to God and yield to his will because he will restore balance and order to our lives. He said, "Come to me, all you who are weary and burdened, and I will give you rest. Take my yoke upon you and learn from me, for I am gentle and humble in heart, and you will find rest for your souls. My yoke is easy, and my burden is light" (Matt 11: 28–30).

The holiday season reminded us that "when the right time came, God sent his Son, born of a woman subject to the Law" (Gal 4:4).

And we understand that the right time always comes. Sometimes we feel God is silent, but give it a second thought if you think that way. You know he is not absent because he is active in our lives. We're all witnesses, as spoken in Jer 29:11: "For I know the plans I have for you," declares the Lord, "plans to prosper you and not to harm you, plans to give you hope and a future."

Think of some circumstances in 2020 or 2021 that smoothed the rough edges of your character and shaped your life. If you did not feel it, you saw it in someone else: your child, sibling, mother, father, cousin, or extended family member. You observed it. Now he sends a new year and speaks again with the simple message that he wants us to be one of his spokespersons in this broken, pandemic-filled world. Be his representative as one of his disciples.

We see God commanding our attention with more pandemics while calling us to consider the needs of others. We read, "They all ate and were filled; and they took up that which remained over of the broken pieces, twelve baskets full and fed five thousand" (Matt 14:20). Like this, we know of God's many miracles. We witness them every day as he still fills the void and emptiness in our lives. We must listen and let him do with our lives as he pleases.

Someone once said, "The only thing that doesn't change in a forever-changing world is change itself." I'm afraid I have to disagree. God never changes. If you're a believer, God is not a stranger to you, and you have a relationship with him. He's in your heart. If he's not, remember him speaking, "Here I am! I stand at the door and knock. If anyone hears my voice and opens the door, I will come in and eat with them, and they will eat with me" (Rev 3:20).

Let us begin our new year with the Lord's Prayer:

> Our Father, who art in heaven, hallowed be thy name; thy kingdom come; thy will be done; on earth as it is in heaven. Give us this day our daily bread. And forgive our trespasses, as we forgive those who trespass against us. And lead us not into temptation; but deliver us from

evil. For thine is the kingdom, the power, and the glory, forever and ever. Amen. (Matt 6:9-13)

Love With or Without the Pandemic

The word "love" appears more than 750 times in the New Living Translation Bible, referring to God's love, familial love, romantic love, and the love shown between brothers and sisters in Christ. Love is a solid feeling of emotional attachment, intense attraction, or profound likability. Covid-19 has shown us the need for love.

First Cor 13:4–8 says, "Love is patient and kind; love does not envy or boast; it is not arrogant or rude. It does not insist on its way; it is not irritable or resentful; it does not rejoice at wrongdoing but with the truth. Love bears all things, believes all things, hopes all things, and endures all things."

Everyone has a definition of love. Romantic love is the magic between two people; only they can describe how they feel toward each other.

Here are several ways in which we can express our love to others as we stay in place or 6 feet apart:

- Listen more attentively and talk less to allow others to share their thoughts and feelings.

- Say "please" and "thank you" to express gratitude for the honor of serving or being served.

- Tell your loved ones how much you love them. Saying the word "love" is meaningful. It takes the guesswork out of taking people for granted.

- Perform an act of service to help someone in need, such as an elderly or disabled individual.

- Give someone a gift from your arsenal—your favorite dessert, brunch, dinner at a local restaurant, or a particular home-cooked meal as a surprise.

- Express other words of love that offers compliments or praise or show affection, gratitude, or encouragement.

- Be present for someone who is physically ill or mourning a death.

- When appropriate, reach out and touch someone's hand or give them a hug or kiss.

- Write a letter or send a card to someone you love. We appreciate this—more favored than sending a text or email.

- Write a love poem that reviews the past or foretells the future according to you or another author; these are read with joy, especially if forgiveness is necessary.

- Apply love to your actions. Like other feelings, expressing love takes practice.

It's important to remember that love shows up in many forms. We can love our pets, family members, friends, and significant others.

Many people believe that love can solve problems. Like the well-known singers the Capitols, Deon Jackson, and Barbara Lewis have recorded, "Love makes the world go round." Love is a universal language.

If you have experienced romantic love, you feel magic in the air when you're with a particular person. That person becomes your world, and everything seems more manageable when they're around. There's something special about your feelings toward them as if your two hearts beat as one. You care deeply for each other.

Whether in a romantic relationship or not, now during the pandemic is an excellent time to honor the concept of love. Love begets love and is, indeed, contagious.

Spiritually speaking, "Let love and faithfulness never leave you; bind them around your neck, write them on the tablet of your heart. Then you will win favor and a good name in the sight of God and man" (Prov 3:3–4).

CHAPTER 4

Faith, Patience, and Prayer

"My faith is in you. Show me your glory.
Breathe life into my indwelling spirit.
I'll press through the crowd, and
you'll know I'm there by my faith."

1. "Now faith is confidence in what we hope for and assurance about what we do not see" (Heb 11:1).

    Prayer: Heavenly Father, we ask you to hear our prayers and guide us. We search for wisdom, love, and compassion for others outside our circle of family and friends. Please help us. We hide the deepest desires of our hearts because we believe in you. We continue asking for life without the pandemic and civility for people. Come quickly, Lord. Let thy will be done. Amen.

2. "This is the confidence we have in approaching God: that if we ask anything according to his will, he hears us. And if we know that he hears us—whatever we ask—we know that we have what we asked of him" (1 John 5:14–15).

    Prayer: Heavenly Father, we come before you asking for answers to our prayers according to your will. We trust that you will respond to whatever we ask if we abide in your word, as in the Bible. We believe you have truly listened and will attend to our prayers for those who are mourning friends and family who passed from the coronavirus. Please let us hear from heaven and show us the healing of our land. Grant this world a better place to live as we awaken to brighter days as you continue to cover all the earth. We give you thanks in advance for we believe your answer is coming. Amen.

3. Wait for the Lord; be strong and take heart and wait for the Lord" (Ps 27:14).

   Prayer: Heavenly Father, COVID-19 test results are impacting our economy, employment, and schools, harming families' livelihoods. We pray that government money will come soon to help the people in need. We trust you to be our refuge as we endure this pandemic worldwide. Give us patience as we wait for the end of this coronavirus season. Help us be strong and take heart as we wait for you, Lord. Send a cure that will heal all individuals who are sick. We thank you in advance for ending COVID-19 from the world. Amen.

4. "In the same way, the Spirit helps us in our weaknesses. We do not know what we ought to pray for, but the Spirit himself intercedes for us through wordless groans. And he who searches our hearts knows the mind of the Spirit because the Spirit intercedes for God's people following the will of God" (Rom 8:26–27).

   Prayer: Heavenly Father, we pray the Lord's Prayer, knowing that God will care for us, forgive us, and do his will on earth. My heart is heavy as we've been praying for our country's leaders, increasing crime and violence, and the spirit of anger and vengeance that we feel for one reason or another among people. We continue to ask, how shall we pray? We don't even understand what our secret hopes should be at these times. Intercede, Lord, you know our hearts. We pray for healing, peace, calm, and justice after you end the pandemic. Amen.

5. "Call on me and come and pray to me, and I will listen to you. You will seek me and find me when you seek me with all your heart. I will be found by you" (Jer 29:12–14).

Prayer: Heavenly Father, we're calling on you in prayer to hear our voices loudly screaming for enough vaccines for the United States and to share with countries in need. We're asking for an end to the pandemic in your way that will bring forth herd immunity. We're requesting an increase in healthcare workers and a decrease in hospitalized patients. Finally, we call on you to implement your new plan for this world. Please help us let go of the pandemic season so we can cling to fresh new beginnings. We welcome your dwelling place among us. Amen.

Afterword

What happened?

IT'S A NEW DAY. The pandemic is a contagious flu. Wars are going on around the world. Inflation is endangering our finances. The job market has changed because nobody wants to work like we used to. It's a new day, so let's continue journal-keeping.

My Faith

The joy of the Lord rests within my faith.

He knew my ending before my beginning.

Everyone receives a measure of faith.

The door opens, and no man has the strength to close it.

Give me all the promises from your word.

My faith is in you. Show me your glory.

Breathe life into my indwelling spirit.

I'll press through the crowd, and

You'll know I'm there by my faith.[1]

The End

---

1. Gwendolyn Carole Tipton, *Feeling Wheels: Poetic Messages of Celebration Reflection, and Emotions* (Bloomington, IN: Xlibris, 2014), 161.

www.ingramcontent.com/pod-product-compliance
Lightning Source LLC
Chambersburg PA
CBHW070737030726
47601CB00001B/46